D0906049

Crossing London's River

Books by John Pudney include:

Non-fiction:

The Smallest Room
The Seven Skies
The Golden Age of Steam
Suez: De Lesseps' Canal

Novels:

The Net
Trespass in the Sun
Thin Air
The Long Time Growing Up

Poetry:

Collected Poems
Spill Out
Spandrels
Take This Orange

Crossing London's River

The bridges, ferries and tunnels crossing the
Thames tideway in London

John Pudney

J M DENT & SONS LTD   LONDON

First published 1972

© John Pudney 1972

All rights reserved. No part of
this publication may be repro-
duced, stored in a retrieval
system, or transmitted, in any
form or by any means, elec-
tronic, mechanical, photocopy-
ing, recording or otherwise,
without the prior permission
of J. M. Dent & Sons Ltd

Made in Great Britain
at the
Aldine Press · Letchworth · Herts
for
J. M. DENT & SONS LTD
Aldine House · Bedford Street · London

ISBN: 0 460 04000 6

Contents

List of Illustrations

IN TEXT

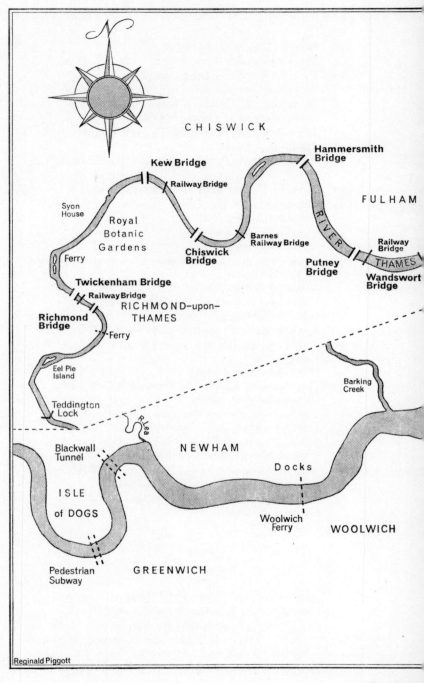

N

CHISWICK

Kew Bridge

Railway Bridge

Hammersmith
Bridge

Syon
House

Royal
Botanic
Gardens

FULHAM

Ferry

Chiswick
Bridge

Barnes
Railway Bridge

RIVER

Railway
Bridge

THAMES

Twickenham Bridge

Putney
Bridge

Wandswort
Bridge

Railway Bridge

Richmond
Bridge

RICHMOND-upon-
THAMES

Ferry

Eel Pie
Island

Barking
Creek

Teddington
Lock

R. Lea

NEWHAM

Blackwall
Tunnel

Docks

ISLE
of DOGS

Woolwich
Ferry

WOOLWICH

Pedestrian
Subway

GREENWICH

Reginald Piggott

Crossings c

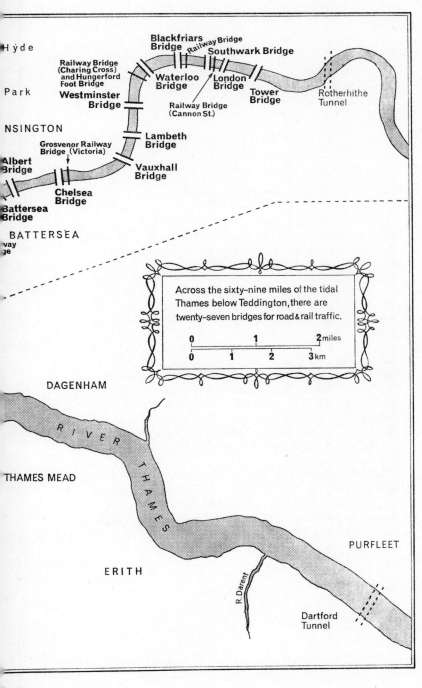

Hȳde

Park

NSINGTON

Railway Bridge (Charing Cross) and Hungerford Foot Bridge

Westminster Bridge

Blackfriars Bridge

Railway Bridge

Southwark Bridge

Waterloo Bridge

London Bridge

Railway Bridge (Cannon St.)

Tower Bridge

Rotherhithe Tunnel

Grosvenor Railway Bridge (Victoria)

Lambeth Bridge

Albert Bridge

Vauxhall Bridge

Chelsea Bridge

Battersea Bridge

BATTERSEA

vay ͻe

Across the sixty-nine miles of the tidal Thames below Teddington, there are twenty-seven bridges for road & rail traffic.

0		1		2 miles
0	1	2		3 km

DAGENHAM

RIVER THAMES

THAMES MEAD

ERITH

R. Darent

PURFLEET

Dartford Tunnel

Thames

Acknowledgments

Without the help of Mr David Leggatt, FLA, former Borough Librarian and Curator at Greenwich, and his staff, this work could not have been written. The author also gratefully acknowledges the help of Mr Roger Osborn of the Corporation of London; Mr D. A. Dawe and Mr Ralph Hyde of the Guildhall Library; Mr H. H. Buckley, the Superintending Engineer and Bridge Master, the Tower Bridge; Mr Barnett G. Wilson, Clerk to the Company of Watermen & Lightermen; Capt. F. L. Millns, general manager, Dartford Tunnel; Mr E. H. Fowkes, Archivist, British Railways Board; and Mr W. B. Caisley of Thames Launches Ltd. The library and information services of the GLC and of all the boroughs on the tideway have also been most constructively helpful and are collectively thanked.

The opening lines of 'The Dry Salvages' from *Four Quartets* by T. S. Eliot, quoted on page 2, are reprinted by permission of Faber and Faber Ltd; and passages from *Locomotion in Victorian London* by G. E. Sekon by permission of Oxford University Press.

1

Crossings

There is this river, from Thames Head to the Nore only just over double the length of the Suez Canal yet so burdened and fringed with history that it defies the compass of any single book. The tidal reaches, sixty-nine miles in length, serve Greater London, and this tideway is crossed by a somewhat haphazard pattern of bridges, tunnels and ferries, a crossing system which is far from systematic, having emerged piece by piece from expediency, from private speculation and, during the last one hundred years or so, from local authority and government effort. The collective existence of these crossings has always been vital to London and to the nation yet they have not often been considered as a whole. In all their disparity they fall into place here and there in the pages of the vast literature of the Thames without ever being accorded a volume to themselves—which they seem to deserve and which we now offer.

London is there because of the river. London was first built on a bluff of high ground on the north bank, with marsh or river on three sides, directly facing a spur of dry land on the south bank. This was a good place for a crossing, the first possible site as you went upstream for a bridge. So it was the attraction of a navigable river that brought settlers to the area and the security of a good crossing which fixed the place. There are thus two themes which have run together and against one another for nearly two thou-

sand years as part of the untidy and fortuitous structure of London
life and history—how to ride the ebb and flow of the river to
advantage and how to cope with it as an obstacle. There is this
conflict between those who navigate the river and those who
need to cross it. In these pages we are concerned with both
because they are inseparable as the twin elements of communication. London is what it is because of this communication serving
strategy, trade, government, civilization and social need. These
elements of communication are individually static. They have
constantly changed while the river basically changes little.

The river is used, regulated but never tamed. Roman engineers
built embankments, twentieth-century technicians plan tidal
barriers: there remains a powerful quality evoked by T. S. Eliot:

> I do not know much about gods; but I think that the river
> Is a strong brown god—sullen, untamed and intractable,
> Patient to some degree, at first recognized as a frontier;
> Useful, untrustworthy, as a conveyor of commerce;
> Then only a problem confronting the builder of bridges.
> The problem once solved, the brown god is almost forgotten
> By the dwellers in cities—ever, however, implacable,
> Keeping his seasons and rages, destroyer, reminder
> Of what men choose to forget. Unhonoured, unpropitiated
> By worshippers of the machine, but waiting, watching and
>   waiting.

There are times when it seems that the 'brown god' is almost
forgotten. The latter end of this century has seen dramatic diminishment in the commercial and social life which rode the ebb and
flow of the tides. Trading and industrial London seems to have
turned its back to the river yet the tideway remains conspicuous,
potent, polluted, beautiful, meandering capriciously, moulding
the metropolis, shaping Greater London. Millions cross and re-
cross it daily regarding it, if at all, as a trifling obstacle rather than
as a hazard. The crossings which have been created individually,
not made to match or complement one another, have rarely been
adequate in the eyes of those who used them. While the metropolis continues to spread and traffic increases in weight and
quantity the crossings will never be adequate. The river crossings
have always had to catch up with demand. The first stone-built

London Bridge was the only bridge serving the citizens for over five centuries, the building of other bridges being held back by vested interests. Its successor, the Rennie Bridge, now shipped across the Atlantic, lasted only just over one hundred and thirty-five years. The 1972 bridge possesses all the qualities which this century's technical skills can bestow but its capacity is no solution in itself to metropolitan traffic congestion, nor can it be regarded as a significant part of a master plan. It is there because London Bridge needed rebuilding. It is individual, singular and, fortunately, good to look at.

The bridges seen individually, or sometimes in groups, are pleasing to the eye and have pleased some notable painters though none of them, except for the well-organized exuberance of the Tower Bridge, were built to beautify the tideway or specifically to enhance London. Charing Cross railway bridge is a Victorian outrage set on a majestic sweep of river unequalled in any European city. Richmond Bridge retains its basic eighteenth-century grace against the green splendours of Richmond Hill. As a modest Victorian effort the Albert suspension bridge possesses special charm. This century has no need to be ashamed of Sir Giles Gilbert Scott's Waterloo Bridge or of the new London Bridge. From an aesthetic as well as a utilitarian point of view the bridges offer diversity and separate grace rather than any general sweep of satisfaction.

The tunnels which began at that part of the tideway where the bridges left off have obviously less potential for glamour though they can be rewarding. The older Brunel's tunnel which killed so many of its builders, nearly drowned his renowned son, and accommodated Queen Victoria, can be viewed from a London underground train in transit between Rotherhithe and Wapping where a little of the original stonework is still visible. Blackwall Tunnel, a late Victorian work, has in the second half of this century been doubled in size and tricked out with handsome motorway approaches. Dartford Tunnel, the most easterly crossing of the broadening tideway with its wide approaches, service buildings and equipment, is a pleasing example of 1960s design. At the other extreme, to the west of the Tower Bridge, Barlow's foot subway lingers on as a ghost tunnel full of pipes with access only by appointment and the turning of rusty, rarely used locks.

The Thames bred its own men, watermen, lightermen, bargemen and ferrymen, who plied their special skills upon the tideway and whose lives and livelihoods were regulated and protected by their guild. There were ferries before bridges. The river banks of the metropolis were thick with ferrymen's stairs during the centuries when London Bridge stood alone, and they lingered on into the age of steam to be cherished by the pen of Charles Dickens. Though the stairs have vanished, to be recalled only in street names, there are ferries still, with histories going back to monastic England but with modern machinery to drive them.

The oars have long since gone with the sails. Steam came and went. Ferry crossings diminished and bridge and tunnel crossings multiplied as London ceased to rely solely upon the tideway for supply and communication. The river is no longer a national thoroughfare and it is the crossing of it that matters. The age-old conflict between what goes across and what goes with the tides finds a somewhat sad solution in a virtually deserted tideway in inner London. London Bridge is built again but there are no more ocean-going vessels to be viewed over its parapet in the Pool of London. The old docks were closing by the 1970s and the commerce of the Pool was moving farther and farther downstream.

When the Romans gave London its name they favoured the place of course as a crossing rather than a port. They laid out Watling Street from the Channel across Kent into Southwark and continued it from their Londinium stronghold to St Albans and the north. Thousands of Roman coins and medallions found in the bed of the river when Old London Bridge was replaced in the eighteen thirties suggest that they built a timber bridge between Southwark and the City, as well as making use of various ferries.

The original Roman thinking on a river crossing serving long-range traffic rather than the terminal needs of a capital city became curiously obscured during the nineteenth century, when so many Thames bridges were built or re-built and when the capital was sprawling in all directions but most convulsively toward the south. The Victorian railroad builders were obsessed only with bringing passengers and goods to London to stop dead at the first convenient terminal point.

Only I. K. Brunel seemed to think further. When he first formulated his plans for the Great Western Railway, his original drawings, which are still to be seen in British Railway archives, envisaged a terminus not at Paddington but in the vicinity of Vauxhall Bridge. This would have given immediate access to the railway systems of the south connecting with the Channel ports. It was a Roman touch, but defeated at the time by vested interests.

The invading Romans themselves lost no time in assessing the strategic value of London as the first point at which a permanent crossing of the river could be made. Ferry crossings in the lower tidal reaches were certainly possible and were used by the ancient Britons and indeed by the Romans, but not for the transportation of armies, military supplies and later the heavy traffic of commerce. For such purposes the geography of Londinium offered the best facilities for regular ferry services and for a bridge.

Before this crossing was substantiated the campaigning Roman armies, like their British opponents, resorted to fords—and fords are an aspect of river-crossing which have always lent themselves to controversy.

Julius Caesar contributed to this by not being very specific in his own account of his campaign of July 54 B.C.:

> Having ascertained their policy, Caesar led his army to the River Thames in the country of Cassivellaunus; which river can be crossed on foot in one place only and that with difficulty. When he came to that place he saw large forces of the enemy drawn up on the opposite bank of the river (which) bank had been fortified by sharp-headed stakes; and stakes of the same sort fixed under the water were covered by the river. Caesar having learnt these things from captives and deserters, (and) having sent the cavalry in advance, ordered the legions to follow with haste, but the soldiers advanced with such speed and impetuosity though their heads only were above water that the enemy could not withstand the assault of the legions and cavalry, but quitted the banks and betook themselves to flight.

Though the river has altered its course in the Brentford/Kew district as in many others over the years and its embankment has removed the possibility of fording, that area has remained the most feasible place for crossing the river bed by foot even in our own time. For instance, Mr J. C. Humphries, the last ferryman to ply at one penny a time between Ferry Lane, Brentford, and Kew Gardens, told the writer that it was possible to walk across the river on stepping-stones occasionally at low tide during the summer months. He recalls that a narrow channel was dredged in the middle of the river bed for the passage of steamers. This formed a ditch across which he could lay his ferry boat as a bridge. 'The year that Windsor Lad won the Derby [1934] I sat in my boat and took the pennies of those who crossed the river.'

Mr Humphries' evidence of a walk-across does not prove anything specific about Caesar's initial crossing. Possibly the Romans used fords in several places. Undoubtedly there have been circumstances from time to time when fords were briefly practical. The *Gentleman's Magazine*, commenting in 1846 on Roman activities stated: 'Even now, in similar seasons [two dry summers consecutively], the river is fordable at Westminster, as it was on the 19th of this very month, July. . . .' In Maitland's 'London', on the same subject the writer states:

> Sounding the river at several neap tides, from Wandsworth to London Bridge, I discovered a ford [on 18th September 1732] about 90 feet west of the S.W. angle of Chelsea College garden, whose channel, in a right line from N.E. to S.W., was no more than 4 feet 7 inches deep, where the day before (it blowing hard from the west) my waterman informed me that the water there was above a foot lower; and it is probable that at such tides, before the course of the river was obstructed either by banks or bridges, it must have been considerably shallower.

The Romans clearly would have preferred ferries to the uncertainties of fords in the long run. With their experience too of bridge-building on the Rhine and other European rivers it is probable they were responsible for the first London Bridge during their period of consolidation following the arrival of Agricola in A.D. 78.

After their departure the existence of London as a stronghold and port was at first a tribal concern of military rather than commercial significance. Then with increasing security, considerations of trade began to emerge. The Anglo-Saxons were interested in moulding the surging tidal sprawl of the river to advantage. A bridge at London and ferries at many points upon the tideway were established. A more secure way of life and trade rested very much upon the settlement and ownership of land, and of the river itself.

The tideway with which this book is concerned runs from the Nore to Teddington Lock, where the tide is brought to a halt. Above this point the river is now administered by the Thames Conservancy. Below, where the tidal river flows through twenty-seven bridges, the river, but not the bridges themselves, is administered by the Port of London Authority. This division of authority was established in 1909.

Basically the Thames is owned by the Crown. At what moment in history this was established it is difficult to decide but the earliest edicts concerned with the management of the river are royal. King Ethelred (866–871) issued a decree about London Bridge: 'Whoever shall come to the bridge in a boat, in which there are fish, he himself being a dealer, shall pay one half-penny for toll, and if it be a larger vessel, one penny.' Edward the Confessor in 1065 decreed: 'If mills, fisheries, or other works are constructed to their [the royal rivers'] hindrance, let these works be destroyed, the waters repaired, and the forfeit to the King not forgotten.' When Richard I handed over the custody of the Thames to the Mayor and Corporation of London, his charter, for which the enormous sum of £20,000, changed hands, included this declaration: 'Know ye all that we, for the health of our soul, our father's soul, and all our ancestors' souls, and also for the common weal of our City of London, and of all our realm have granted and steadfastly commanded that all weirs that are in the Thames be removed, wheresoever they shall be within the Thames. . . . For it is manifest to us . . . that great detriment and inconvenience hath grown to our said City of London, and also to the whole realm, by occasion of the said weirs.'

Before the reign of Queen Elizabeth I there had been no suggestion that the Crown owned the foreshores of the kingdom generally but after her accession claims were made both to the foreshore between high and low water mark throughout the realm and to any land which had at any time been subject to the flux and reflux of the sea. King James I saw great opportunities for profit in this. He appointed Commissioners who sold 'for ready money to be paid in hand' the foreshore rights to the various owners of riverside property, and this business thrived.

With the passing of the Crown Lands Management Act 1829 the Commissioners of Woods and Forests revived the Crown's claims to the foreshore, which had lain dormant for many years. In 1844 the Attorney-General filed an information against the Corporation of London concerning proprietary rights over the foreshores of the Thames. The case dragged on for more than a decade and the outcome was an agreement between the Crown and the Corporation by which a grant was made in 1857 of all the interest in the bed and soil of the Thames within the flux and reflux of the tide. This was confirmed by the Act of 1857 creating the Thames Conservancy. From that time the Thames Conservancy controlled the whole of the river until the formation of the Port of London Authority in 1909.

The establishment of the ferries, bridges and tunnels had this legal background. The ferries being the oldest have origins which are obscure though their regulation was clearly defined from the earliest times. 'The owner of the ferry', wrote F. M. Fuller, Chief Engineer to the LCC, 'need not be the owner of the land on either side of the water, but he is bound to maintain safe boats and employ fit persons as ferrymen. In return, he can charge tolls and has a right of action against those who disturb his franchise or diminish his custom by setting up a new ferry.'

Bridges like ferries were initiated and run by private enterprises, which were bought out. It was of course the ratepayers of London who ultimately bore the burden of these transactions. Only London Bridge itself, the forerunner of all the bridges, was conceived in its earlier days as an affair of national significance and pride though it charged for its services until the middle of the eighteenth century. Its financial arrangements are unique. It is self-supporting, having what amounts to a private income. This is now shared with the Tower, Southwark and Blackfriars Bridges though it emanates from the first stone-built bridge begun in 1176 and demolished in 1832. The citizens of medieval London from the thirteenth century onwards contributed to their bridge and remembered it in their wills. Thus one Johanna Bytheweye in 1300 left 'to the work of London Bridge twelve pence'. A year later Margery Bacheler bequeathed her gold wedding ring to the bridge. Some left a mere sixpence—a more significant sum then than now. Some, like one Richard Baconn in 1363, made the substantial bequest of 100 marks. The capital and revenues of the bridge increased with the years, administered as a trust from medieval times till the present day by the Bridge House Estates, a department of the Corporation of London. The income is impressive. In 1969–70 it was £890,600 and the excess of gross income over expenditure was £697,535.

No other bridge in the world has a more diverse or better documented history, which has been faithfully preserved in the Bridge House offices. Here one can view the ancient leases written on parchment of those who lived and traded on the bridge, going back to the thirteenth century. The only obscurity concerns the origins of the early timber bridges on the site. We simply have to begin by knowing that a bridge was there.

2

Old London Bridge

London Bridge was there, not always precisely in the same spot, for the best of all reasons. Geographically it was right at a time when the river was quite untamed, running tidally through acres of marsh and thousands of creeks. Strategically it suited the Romans, and for the Anglo-Saxons it was an extension of the fortification of London. Commercially it became both a gateway of trade and a part of the structure of a port. It acquired prestige and ceremonial significance. For many centuries indeed it was a wonder of the civilized world, hospitable, cruel, frivolous, menacing by turns and expensive but never a luxury. Glamour with singularity diminished in the eighteenth century. The last century swept it away physically and replaced it partly in the interests of steam navigation, which in turn the twentieth century swept away.

From the time of the Romans till the tenth century some sort of timber bridge existed. It may well have collapsed from time to time and been replaced. The first specific reference to its existence is not very edifying. It is the record of the judicial drowning of a supposed witch. In the Anglo-Saxon records this poor woman, a widow, is not named. Her alleged victim was one Aelsie described as father of Wulfstane. The widow was caught driving iron pins into an effigy of Aelsie: 'Then they took that woman and drowned her at London Bridge and her son escaped and was outlawed and the land was forfeited to the King. . . .'

This is the only reference to the use of the bridge as a place of execution though it later enjoyed a long and grisly vogue as a place for the display of the heads of executed people. Most of the early historical records which follow show the bridge to have played a role in the defence of London which was every bit as significant as its use as a crossing. When for instance Cnut sailed his Viking fleet up from Greenwich to attack the city he found the defended bridge impassable. He therefore cut ditches and enlarged existing waterways through the marshes in the Southwark area in an attempt to by-pass the bridge.

There is a dramatic account in *Heimskringla* of the pitched battle for the bridge in the reign of Aethelred (978–1016):

The same autumn that King Olaf came to England, it happened that King Swend [Sweyn] died suddenly in the night in his bed; and it is said by Englishmen that Edmund the Saint killed him. . . . When Aethelred, the King of the English, heard this in Flanders, he returned directly to England and no sooner was he come back, than he sent an invitation to all men who would enter into his pay, to join him in recovering the country. Then many people flocked to him; and among others came King Olaf with a great troop of Northmen to his aid. They steered first to London, and sailed into the Thames with their fleet; but the Danes had a castle within. On the other side of the river is a great trading place, which is called Suthvirki [Southwark]. There the Danes had raised a great work, dug large ditches, and within had built a bulwark of stone, timber and turf, where they had stationed a strong army. King Aethelred ordered a great assault; but the Danes defended themselves bravely, and King Aethelred could make nothing of it. Between the castle and Suthvirki there was a bridge, so broad that two waggons could pass each other upon it. On the bridge were raised barricades, both towers and wooden parapets in the direction of the river, which were nearly breast high; and under the bridge were piles driven into the bottom of the river. Now when the attack was made the troops stood on the bridge everywhere, and defended themselves. King Aethelred was very anxious to get possession of the bridge, and he called together all the chiefs to consult how they should get the bridge broken down. Then said King Olaf he would attempt to lay his fleet alongside of it, if the other ships would do the same. It was then determined in this council that they should lay their war forces under the bridge; and each made himself ready with ships and men. King Olaf ordered great platforms of floating wood to be tied together with hazel bands, and for this he took down old houses; and with these, as a roof, he covered over the ships' sides. Under this screen he set pillars so high and stout, that there both was room for swinging their swords, and the roofs were strong enough to withstand the stones cast down upon them. Now when the fleet and men were ready, they rowed up along the river; but when they came near the bridge, there were cast down upon them so many stones and missile weapons, such as arrows and spears, that neither helmet not shield could hold against it; and the ships themselves were so greatly damaged that many retreated out of it. But King Olaf, and the Northmen's fleet with him, rowed quite up under the bridge, laid their cables around the piles which supported it, and then rowed off with all the ships as hard as they could down the stream. The piles were thus shaken in the bottom and were loosened under the bridge. Now as the armed troops stood thick upon the bridge, and there were likewise many heaps of stones and other weapons upon it being loosened and broken, the bridge gave way; and a great part of the men upon it fell into the river, and all the others fled, some into the castle, some into Southwark. Thereafter Southwark was stormed and taken. Now when the people in the castle saw that the river Thames was mastered and that they could not hinder the passage of ships up into the country, they became afraid, surrendered the tower and took Aethelred to be their king.

From this affray came the famous nursery rhyme 'London Bridge is broken down'. The words have been varied according to taste and circumstances over the years. The translation by Samuel Laing of the original by Ottar Svarte in the Olaf Sagas goes like this:

> London Bridge is broken down
> Gold is won, and bright renown
> Shields resounding,
> War-horns sounding,
> Hildur shouting in the din!
> Arrows singing,
> Mailcoats ringing—
> Odin makes our Olaf win!
>
> King Aethelred has found a friend:
> Brave Olaf will his throne defend—
> In bloody fight
> Maintain his right

Win back his land
With blood-red hand
And Edmund's son upon his throne replace—
Edmund, the star of every royal race!

Some of the fire and fury went out of the words in the course of
time. Londoners celebrated the construction of their first stone
bridge with

Build it up with stone so strong
Dance over my Lady Lee.
Hazza, 'twill last for ages long
With a gay ladee.

A later version by Henry Carey, who wrote the words of 'God Save
the King', begins 'London Bridge is broken down, My fair lady'.

During the following 150 years the bridge was twice destroyed
and twice rebuilt. Most of London, like the bridge, was timber-
built and between 1077 and 1136 eight great fires swept through
the city, all of which caused some damage to the bridge. In
Norman times the cost of its repair and maintenance became a
grievous burden not only upon Londoners but upon the people
of neighbouring counties. The *Anglo-Saxon Chronicle* of 1097
states that 'many counties that were confined to London by work
were grievously oppressed on account of the wall they were
building about the Tower and the bridge that was nearly all
afloat'.

In 1091 a great storm struck the city, destroying some 600
houses and causing a great flooding of the river. Such a quantity
of wreckage and timber came down that London Bridge was
virtually swept away. Only two years later heavy autumn rains
were followed by severe frost and the river was frozen over. Horses
and wagons crossed over the ice. When the thaw came the wooden
bridge was again almost destroyed by the pressure of floating ice.

The repair of the bridge under the Normans sometimes entailed
the use of forced labour. The first record of an individual expert
occurs in 1130, when Geoffrey, 'Ingeniator', was paid £25 for the
construction of 'two arches of London Bridge'. By that time the
bridge had already received some endowments and there is every

likelihood that these would have been administered by the clergy as acts of piety. The clergy in any case were the only educated people in the Middle Ages and would tend to be in charge of any civil as opposed to military construction work. The Church throughout Europe was associated with bridge-building. The bridge at Avignon was the work of the Frères Pontifes, who had originated in Italy, and this fraternity which became known as the order of Saint-Jacques-du-Haut-Pas was widely revered for its work in bridge-building and the maintenance of ferries. It was not surprising therefore that a priest emerged as a bridge-builder in London. In 1163 the last of the timber bridges was completed in elm under the direction of Peter the Bridge Master who was also Chaplain of St Mary Colechurch—the church in which Thomas Becket had been baptized, a connection which was to have some significance in the history of London Bridge. Peter was the head of a fraternity similar to the Frères Pontifes. Later, when the bridge had been dedicated to Becket's memory, they became known as the Fraternity of St Thomas, but they were also described variously in the bridge records as the 'Master and Brethren of the Bridge of London', 'Chaplains, Brethren and Sisters of the Bridge of London', and as 'Brethren and Proctors of London Bridge'.

The knowledge, technical skill and organizing ability of Peter de Colechurch were evidently matched by an exceptional talent for raising and administering a force of expert builders, for in about 1176 he began the construction of a stone bridge which was to serve London for over six centuries. It took more than thirty years to build, while its predecessor continued in everyday use,

The priest builder must have been influential and persuasive to press relentlessly forward with his imaginative and unique design. No doubt he pointed out how frequently the timber bridges had suffered from fire and flood. No doubt arguments for defence came into it, for his structure was to be a fortified approach to the city centre both by land and by water. There was not much precedent to go on except for some stone bridges built by the Romans on the Continent, which were still in use at that time though their construction had not been imitated. It sometimes happens that similar inventions and innovations spring up spontaneously unrelated to one another in quite separate parts of the world—as did radio and hovercraft development in our own time. So it seems that about the time that Peter de Colechurch set to work in London, St Benézét was starting his great bridge of twenty-three broad arches across the Rhône at Avignon.

Peter's bridge consisted of a stone platform which has been variously recorded as being between 880 and 936 feet long—though several eighteenth-century architects surveyed it, none of their measurements agree. The original width, according to Gordon Home, was 20 feet though this has been given as 40 feet by some writers. It contained a drawbridge and nineteen broad-pointed arches, which varied in width from 17 feet 9 inches to 26 feet 6 inches. There were massive piers which were called starlings, built out to protect the footings of the arches. The water raced back and forth between these for the bridge was virtually a weir, reducing a channel of some 900 feet to a number of waterways totalling just over 190 feet.

The width of the timber drawbridge opening was only 28 feet 7 inches, brought down by the starlings to about 20 feet clear for the passage of larger ships making for the city's main port at Queenhithe. The significance of this was stressed by Stow: '. . . what time the timber bridge of London was drawn up, for the passage of them to the said Hithe, as to a principall strand for landing and unloading against the middest and hart of the Citie.'

Thus the basic conception of Old London Bridge was to serve two purposes. It gave access to a safe and well-sited harbour and conserved above-bridge navigation: and it was the arterial road into the capital with the drawbridge a potent item of defence. To these purposes were added the unique qualities of being at once a bastion and a place of habitation, trade and worship.

How the priest-builder carried out this great work during more than three decades over almost untamed tidal waters has been a matter for wonder and conjecture. Stow's *Survey of London* states that 'the course of the river for the time was turned another way about by a Trench cast for that purpose beginning, as is supposed, East about Radriffe [Ratcliffe], and ending in the West about Patricksey, now tearmed Batersey'. This notion of driving channels through the marshed on the south bank had been attempted

in Anglo-Saxon times with some success by Cnut and his Viking
fleet, though his operation was not a diversion of the river but a
temporary waterway for the navigation of not very large ships. If
the medieval builders had really succeeded in diverting the river
it would have entailed building two great dams, one above and
one below the point of construction. Such a task would have been
too great even for the ingenuity of these twelfth-century builders:
and if anything of the kind had been attempted it would surely
have been recorded. Sir Christopher Wren, quoted by Nicholas
Hawksmoor, seemed to have been quite certain in his mind that
the river was not diverted 'but that every Pier was set upon Piles
of Wood, which were drove as far as might be under low Water-
mark, on which were laid Planks of Timber, and upon them the
Foundation of the Stone Piers'.

As each pier was completed, pinching the width of the river
together, the rush of waters with every tide must have made the
work of pile-driving more and more hazardous. The crossing of
the Thames tideway has taken a heavy toll of human life since
that poor widow was drowned for witchcraft and the first records
were written down. Forty men lost their lives during the construction of Rennie's subsequent London Bridge, which took seven and
a half years to build. As old London Bridge took nearly five times
as long, the death roll among Peter de Colechurch's people may
well have been numbered in hundreds. Though the financial cost
of crossing the river throughout the years is well documented the
cost in human lives goes very little on record.

But while the bridge was still under construction it already
found favour as a grandstand for water sports. Fitz Stephen
writing between 1170 and 1182 mentions the new structure:

> A target is strongly fastened to a trunk or mast fixed in the middle
> of the river, and a youngster standing upright in the stern of a boat
> made to move as fast as the oars and current can carry it, is to
> strike the target with his lance; and if in hitting it he break his
> lance, and keep his place in the boat, he gains his point, and
> triumphs, but if it happen that the lance be not shivered by the
> force of the blow, he is of course tumbled into the water, and
> away goes his vessell without him . . . the Bridge, and the
> balconies on the banks, are filled with spectators, whose business
> it is to laugh.

The stone used for the building was Kentish rag brought up from the Medway area, with additions from the quarries near Merstham in Surrey. The original cost of construction came from existing endowments, from a wool tax imposed by King Henry II and from generous subscriptions such as the thousand marks contributed each by the Archbishop of Canterbury and by the Papal Legate. Undoubtedly Peter de Colechurch suffered from time to time from lack of cash and from difficulty in obtaining the right materials. It is not surprising that the work lasted through several reigns so that this great engineer did not live to see the end of it.

He died in 1205, twenty-five years after his inauguration of the project, and Stow records that four years later, in 1209, the bridge was finished 'by the worthy Marchants of London, Serle Mercer, William Almaine, and Benedict Botewrite . . . principall Maisters of that worke'. Peter de Colechurch was buried in the undercroft of the bridge chapel dedicated to the Blessed Martyr St Thomas of Canterbury, the cost of which had been borne by a mason who was the 'Maister Workeman of the Bridge'. The builder-priest's tomb was under a floor of black and white marble beneath the chapel. Some six centuries later workmen demolishing the bridge in 1832 reached the floor of the lower chapel and came upon the unmarked grave. No reference was ever made to the disposal of the priest-builder's remains and, writes Gordon Home, 'we are reluctantly compelled to believe that Londoners, who were then ready enough to do honour to the memory of the designer of their new bridge, destroyed, without giving more than the briefest newspaper paragraphs to record the event, the resting-place and the remains of the pioneer of European fame who first designed and built a great bridge of stone in the British Isles.'

It was not only what went across and beneath Peter de Colechurch's structure, it was what was built upon the bridge itself and the life that went with it which has given London Bridge its unique place in history. Because London Bridge was so celebrated there are fortunately many illustrations at various stages in its history. The first complete representation, now in the Bodleian Library at Oxford, was done by Antony Van den Wyngaerde. Visscher's view made before the Great Fire of 1632–3 with

Southwark Cathedral in the foreground is one of the most detailed and vivacious. It was the subject which attracted among others Claude de Jongh, William Hogarth, Samuel Scott, Antonio Canaletto and J. M. W. Turner. Holbein lodged on the bridge and depicted it but this picture was destroyed in the Great Fire of London of 1666.

From such pictorial records as these we look at one of the busiest scenes in English history. In Elizabethan times the travel writer John Lyly stared in wonder (getting the number of arches wrong): '. . . and among al the straung and beautifull showes me thinketh there is none so notable, as the Bridge which crosseth the Theames, which is in manner of a continuall streete, well replenyshed with large and stately houses on both sides, and situate upon twentie Arches whereof each one is made of excellent free stone squared.' Quite soon after its completion in 1209 the bridge began to acquire a reputation for frailty, and its history has often been described as a narrative of repairs. Nevertheless the building which went up on its superstructure was continuous and ever-changing. Fires raged and destroyed buildings, but never the bridge itself. With changing times and politics the buildings were taken down, remodelled or improved. Life finally drained away from the superstructure, which was becoming more and more dangerous, at the beginning of the eighteenth century, and it was finally demolished between 1758 and 1762.

To the traveller approaching the capital from Southwark the bridge may well have appeared as a bastion of the city. The bridge gate was built as a fortification over the first arches at the Southwark terminus. It was used ineffectually to exclude Simon de Montfort when he marched on the city in the thirteenth century. Though the custodian flung the keys into the river the gates were battered down by de Montfort's supporters within the city. In the fifteenth century the structure like so many of its neighbours fell into disrepair. 'This gate,' writes Stow 'with the tower thereupon, and two arches of the bridge, fell down, and no man perished by the fall thereof, in the year 1436; towards the new building whereof divers charitable citizens gave large sums of money.' It was rebuilt only to be assaulted again in 1471 by Bastard Falconbridge and his men, who burnt it and also destroyed thirteen

houses on the bridge. Three centuries later just before it was
finally demolished a Bridge House Committee stated: 'We find
that the said gate is now but 13 feet wide, and to enlarge the same
so that two carts or coaches may pass through together, the middle
part thereof must be entirely taken down.'

In the years between, this gate was notorious for its display of
the heads of executed traitors impaled on pikes. During the reign
of Henry VIII the severed heads proliferated and achieved two
ugly distinctions. A woman's head appeared—Elizabeth Barton,
the 'Holy Maid of Kent', a visionary who had prophesied that if
the King divorced Katherine and married Anne Boleyn he would
die a villain's death. Then appeared the most distinguished head
of all, that of Sir Thomas More, the author of *Utopia* and former
Lord Chancellor. After More's head had remained on its pole for
some months, according to his great grandson, Cresacre More,
it was bought by his favourite daughter Margaret Roper to
prevent its being thrown into the river to make way for the next
victim and to become 'foode for fishes'. He also declared: 'It was
very well to be knowen, as well by the livelie favour of him, which
was not all this while in anie thing almost diminished; as also by
reason of one tooth which he wanted while he lived: herein it was
to be admired, that the hayres of his head being almost gray,
before his martyrdome, they seemed now, as it were, readish or
yellow.' Certain miraculous qualities were also attributed to
Fisher, Bishop of Rochester, whose severed head preceded that of
More on public exhibition in 1535. According to a biography of
Fisher published more than one hundred years after his death his
head exposed on London Bridge 'grewe daily fresher and fresher,
so that in his life time he never looked so well'. This miracle
caused a traffic jam on the bridge, 'Wherefore the people cominge
daily to see this strange sight, the passage over the bridge was so
stopped with their goinge and comminge, that almost nether Cart
nor horse could passe: And therefore at the end of xiij daies the
Executioner commaunded to throwe downe the heade, in the night
time, into the river of Thames.'

The relics upon the bridge did not weigh heavily upon the mind
of King Henry VIII. We read of him, after Jane Seymour had
been proclaimed Queen at Greenwich, travelling in state upriver

to Westminster. 'And so the Kinge passed throwe London Bridge, with his trumpetts blowinge before him, and shalmes, sagbuttes, and dromeslawes playing also in barges going before him, which was a goodlie sight to beholde.'

To Peter de Colechurch cannot be ascribed any of the savagery which made the bridge a place of exhibition for human remains. His own pious thought was better expressed in the famous chapel which he embodied in his design dedicated to St Thomas of Canterbury, Becket having been canonized only a year or so before the foundations of the bridge were laid. The chapel was the first of the buildings to be erected upon the bridge. It was built on the tenth or centre pier, being 60 feet high, so arranged that there were two chapels one above the other, the upper chapel being at street level and the lower being built into the structure of the bridge itself. At that time when London rivalled Canterbury in its devotion to St Thomas the dedication of this chapel to the London saint was both an imaginative and a shrewd move. The chapel flourished for several hundred years, being rebuilt and refurbished, but with the Reformation first the dedication to St Thomas then the chapel itself were threatened. In 1543 a man received 13s. 4d. for 'altering of the marterdom of Thomas Beckett unto the image of Our Lady'. Six years later a City minute ran 'It is agreid that Mr. Wylford and Mr. Judde, surveyours of the workes of the brydge, shall to-morrowe begyn to cause the chapell upon the same brydge to be defaced, and to be translated into a dwellyng-house, with as moche spede as they convenyentlye maye.' Seventeenth-century drawings and maps show the chapel house in private occupation.

Those who dwelt and traded on London Bridge were noticeably healthier than their fellows. No doubt this was due to the fact that plenty of fresh air reached them from the tideway and that they were clear of the cesspits and choked open drains of London and Southwark. Dr E. Baynard writing in 1709 about the Great Plague states: 'I remember that I heard an Apothecary say (I think it was Mr. Thomas Soaper) who lived then on London Bridge (an ingenious, sober Man) that there were but two Persons died on the Bridge in the whole time of the Visitation. The Truth of this may easily be inquired into, there being many Men now alive, that then lived on the Bridge, or near it. And I have been lately told, by several Eminent Men, living on London-Bridge, that they have observed, that for the quantity of Houses, that the Bridge scapes better than other parts of the City, in any Contagious time whatsoever : . . .'

There were other hazards which were special to the bridge-dwellers. Several occasions are noted in the records when their houses were damaged by shipping. For instance in 1465 a foreign master paid a forfeit of 12*d*. 'for mending the windows of a tenement upon the bridge broken by him with his ship.'

There is no certain record of the first building of the first house, which no doubt followed the building of the chapel, but from the twelfth century the parchments relating to the building, rebuilding and leasing of these tenements have been preserved in the offices of the Bridge House Estates. In 1460 the number of tenements in the different sections of the bridge was set out as follows :

The beginning at the east of the bridge				32
,,	,,	west	,,	31
The middle	,,	east	,,	18
,,	,,	west	,,	18
The end	,,	east	,,	15
,,	,,	west	,,	15

The trades carried on at that time included 'haberdassher, jueller, cultellar, bowyer, armurar, pynner, fleccher, taillour, peyntour and goldsmith'. At a later date there were some notable stationers, publishers and booksellers upon the bridge. It must have been a stimulating place to live and trade, with signs hanging out from all the shops and a stream of traffic both above and below the bridge. During the sixteenth and seventeenth centuries stallholders added to the confusion. A committee in 1580 was formed to deal with the 'reformation of the annoyances of the stalls of the shops on London Bridge . . .' and settle on a limitation of dimensions. In 1658 the Common Council was concerned with traffic problems 'by reason of the irregular passing and repassing of coaches, carts and cars, and the standing of costers and [sic] mongers, and other loose people there, continued stops are made upon the said bridge, whereby several abuses are daily committed there, and the inhabitants very much prejudiced and hindered in the despatch of their business in their several trades.'

Elizabethan times produced a new wonder on London Bridge. When the drawbridge gatehouse was demolished the Lord Mayor in the presence of the sheriffs and bridge masters laid in its place the foundations of Nonesuch House. This remarkable timber-framed building constructed without the use of a single nail was prefabricated in Holland and shipped over in pieces. It spanned the bridge on the city side of the drawbridge, being built on the seventh and eighth arches from the Southwark end. It overhung the parapet on each side leaving a clear passage of twenty feet wide beneath it. This wooden palace upon the bridge was a true emanation of the Renaissance, adorned with turrets at its four corners and crowned with onion-shaped cupolas carrying gilded weather-vanes. There were windows on all sides of it and the whole was richly ornamented and painted. It remained one of the glories of London from 1579 till 1757 when it was ingloriously demolished.

3

Life on Old London Bridge

From the time that people started to live and trade on it, London Bridge became a community with a life of its own. From the Middle Ages until well into the nineteenth century the river itself was every bit as much a thoroughfare as the arterial road which passed over the bridge. The river was also a place of pleasure, pageantry and resort and what went under the bridge continually vied in interest and excitement with what went over the bridge—with a strong spice of danger added, for the 'shooting' of the bridge was often extremely hazardous.

Londoners could add hazards of their own to unpopular figures. When the glamorous but unpopular Eleanor of Provence, 'Elinor la Belle' to the minstrels, consort of Henry III, found the climate of the Tower of London uncongenial in summer she ordered the royal barge to carry her to Windsor: 'The Londoners,' writes Blaauw, in his *Barons' War*, 'assailed her when the barge approached the bridge with every mark of foul indignity and hatred; the rudest curses, the most opprobrious accusations were shouted at her, while mud, broken eggs, and stones were thrown down with so much violence as to compel a retreat to the Tower.'

Queen Eleanor, in keeping with her reputation as the most unpopular queen in Europe, was later revenged on London Bridge. In the last years of his long reign Henry III handed over the bridge revenues to her by edict. 'The King to all . . . greeting. Seeing that sometime since we would have granted to our most dear Consort Eleanor, Queen of England, the Custody of our Bridge at London, with the liberties and all other things belonging to that Bridge, to have for a certain term: We, therefore, do grant to the same Queen, out of our abundant grace and will, the custody of the Bridge aforesaid, with the liberties and all other things belonging to that Bridge, until the Feast of All Saints [1st November] about to arrive; and from the same Feast of All Saints, until the full end of the six years next approaching, and following. In testimony of which thing . . . Witness the King, at Woodstock, on the 10th day of September [1269].' As Queen Mother, Eleanor held on to the money for something like six years from 1272 to 1278, starving the bridge of the revenue needed for its considerable running repairs.

In the fourteenth century the bridge continued to serve its purpose as a bastion not against foreign enemies but in civil strife. Wat Tyler came from Blackheath to set fire to Southwark in 1381. He was checked at London Bridge by William Walworth, mayor, who caused the drawbridge to be raised and 'fastened a great chaine of yron acrosse, to restrain their entry'.

Jack Cade, leading his rebellion in 1450, induced the citizens to open the bridge gates and as he crossed the drawbridge he cut the ropes which supported it with his sword, his crossing being recorded in the words of Shakespeare's Henry VI

> Jack Cade hath gotten London Bridge; the citizens
> Fly and forsake their houses.

Though he overran the city Cade remained based at Southwark, and the bloody battles that ensued to contain the rebels on the south bank took place mostly on the bridge. While many of the houses were set on fire and many non-belligerents, including women and children, lost their lives by fire and drowning, Cade's head eventually was placed on the bridge gate.

One of the most extraordinary events upon London Bridge arose from the banquet given in Scotland in 1389 at which Lord Welles, the English Ambassador, was present and the conversation not unexpectedly turned on the comparative merits of English and Scots. According to Holinshed, Welles issued a challenge to anyone present to meet him in the lists 'with speares sharpe groond for life and death'. Sir David de Lindesay took up the challenge. Welles then insisted that the joust must take place out of Scotland and, for some reason never explained, selected London Bridge. Lindesay, who had the right to select the day, chose St George's Day, 22nd April 1390, and Welles returned to London to obtain a safe conduct for his opponent, which was duly given in these terms:

> Safe conduct for David de Lyndesey, Knight, for the duel to be fought with John de Welles.
> The King to all and singular, our Sheriffs, Mayors, Bailiffs, Ministers, and faithful subjects, within and without our liberties, to whom these present letters shall come, Greeting. Know ye, that because our beloved and faithful John de Welles, for the perfecting of a certain Passage of Arms within our Kingdom of England, against David de Lyndeseye, of Scotland, Knight, as he appears to have been calumniated by the said David—he is petitioner to us for the security of the said David, with his followers and servants coming into our Kingdom aforesaid, for the cause aforesaid, and graciously to provide for their remaining here, and returning again to their own country.

The safe conduct ran for two months, allowing Lindesay a suitable retinue of Knights, Esquires, Varlets and Pages.

King Richard II lived it up in flamboyant style, and when his dais was erected on London Bridge—exactly where on the bridge is not known—the magnificence of the arrangements excelled all pageantry the bridge had ever known. Members of the court and the nobility were assigned to their special positions. The possibilities of any routine traffic crossing the bridge were slight indeed. The Chronicles of Holinshed, themselves deriving from contemporary sources, tell us how heralds gave the signal, the heavily armoured contestants charged, broke their spears and remained seated in their saddles: 'The people beholding how stiffelie . . . David sat without moving, cried that the Scottisman was locked in his saddle. He hearing this, leapt beside his horse, and verie nimblie mounted up againe into the saddle, armed as he was, to the great wonder of the beholders.'

The warriors charged for the second time. Again their spears were splintered but they themselves remained undamaged on their heavy horses. The third clash brought the Englishman, Lord Welles, crashing down on to the cobbles 'sore hurt'.

The gallant Lindesay dismounted and held his opponent in his arms until first aid had been given. His gallantry was undiminished after the event. Every day he visited Welles's bedside and his stay in London was prolonged by permission of the King. Finally he sailed away from London Bridge aboard a Scottish vessel named the *Seinte Marie* and it was ordered that the crew 'were not to carry with them any property or goods whatsoever, nor any illicit goods, or prohibited merchandise out of the kingdom . . . excepting only one complete armour of war for the body of David Lyndesey of Scotland, Knight.' On his return to Scotland Lindesay was created Earl of Crawford and later came back as Ambassador to England.

At the end of the fourteenth century Richard II, through reckless expenditure, came into conflict with the City Fathers over a loan. The outcome of these transactions was that the King imprisoned the Mayor and Sheriffs and levied a fine of £100,000 on the City.

When in August 1392 the King announced his intention of making a progress by road from his palace at Sheen to Westminster, the citizens chose London Bridge as the site for a kind of pageant of appeasement. The King accepted an invitation from the new Mayor and the Bishop of London to 'take so great peyne upon hym as to ryde thoroughe his chaumber of London'. At Southwark the royal procession was met by a great gathering of clergy and choristers. At the bridge gate awaited an assembly of the City Fathers to make a ceremonial presentation of two milk-white horses 'trappyd in ryche cloth of golde', the harness tinkling with silver bells. After the splendours of this crossing of London Bridge the King was duly appeased, remitted the fine and restored the liberties of the City.

Only three years later when Richard had remarried and was bringing home his new consort, the daughter of the King of France, the London Bridge pageantry was repeated after the royal cavalcade had been met at Blackheath by the Mayor and Aldermen clothed in scarlet. But this time the crowds on London

Bridge got out of control and some eight or nine people were crushed to death.

These events are selected from many occasions on which London Bridge, more particularly in the Middle Ages, and sometimes in later years, was used as a ceremonial place for entry into the city or into the realm. The well-documented records of the bridge itself and of the city are full of splendours, not least the triumphal return of Henry V from Agincourt with the French king captive in his train, or the expensive pageant celebrated on the bridge for the arrival of Katharine of Aragon to accept the crown from Henry VIII.

The sixteenth century certainly provides, in the story of Edward Osborne, the strongest romantic element. In the 1530s he was sent from his native Ashford, Kent, to be bound apprentice to a wealthy clothworker on the bridge named William Hewet. In 1536 Hewet's daughter Anne, at play at an upper window, toppled over into the river. Edward the apprentice dived in and saved her. The story comes from Stow's *Survey of London*; it does not give the state of the tide at the time but all circumstances point to the rescue being spectacular, even in the days when drownings were frequent in these dangerous waters. Osborne remained in the household of William Hewet, who became Mayor of London in 1559. Anne grew up and there were many suitors, but Sir William Hewet, as he became, said Osborne saved her and Osborne should enjoy her. He provided a handsome dowry and the wedding took place in 1562.

Osborne prospered and in 1583 he became Sir Edward Osborne, Lord Mayor of London, and he was the first governor of the Turkey Company. The descendants of this romantic marriage steadily climbed in social grandeur until their great-grandson in 1694 was created Duke of Leeds, described not too kindly by John Evelyn as 'a man of excellent natural parts; but nothing of generous or grateful'. Sir Edward Osborne's portrait showing him armour-clad remained in the possession of the Duke of Leeds' family.

The bridge acquired a unique industrial use in the sixteenth century when the tidal flow under the first arch at the city end was first harnessed for raising water. The pioneer was Peter

Morice, a Dutch engineer who claimed that he could supply even those parts of the city which were on higher ground. To demonstrate the effectiveness of his machinery he directed a jet of water over the steeple of a church and was duly granted a lease of one arch for 500 years at ten shillings per annum. There was opposition from the water-bearers of the city but Morice's waterworks hydraulic machinery soon proved its efficiency and a second arch was granted on the same terms in 1582. This enterprise continued in the family, which came to be known as Morris. According to the records of the Company of Watermen, Thomas Morris in 1701 sought permission to erect one or more engines at the fourth arch —the third already being dammed up. He met with some opposition, mainly from those concerned with navigation, but ultimately a lease was granted which added greatly to the value of the family enterprise. A year or so later the family sold out for £36,000 to a goldsmith named Richard Soams, who turned the enterprise into a company of 300 shares at £500 each. In 1767 a fifth arch was acquired in the teeth of opposition from those concerned with navigation, and the waterworks remained in operation until 1822, when an Act was passed for their removal, with £10,000 paid as compensation to the proprietors.

When Peter de Colechurch built the bridge the population of London was probably about 40,000. By 1750 it was over 675,000. In spite of the growth, increased wealth, commercial significance and spread of the city along the banks of the Thames toward the west, no new bridge was built in the metropolitan area until the completion of Westminster Bridge in 1749. Upstream at Putney the first bridge was built in 1729 but in those days Putney was relatively remote and it is an astonishing fact that for nearly five and a half centuries Londoners were served only by the one bridge, which was constantly under repair and frequently closed, and by the innumerable ferries which plied from stairs throughout the city. During these five and a half centuries there was a steady increase in vehicular traffic. Improvements in the road systems and a greater sophistication in wheeled vehicles not only increased commerce but enabled more and more citizens to take up residence and to trade outside the old city boundaries. Already the watermen were complaining that vehicular traffic was affecting their earnings on the river and indeed the Thames was beginning to show signs of diminishing in importance as London's main thoroughfare. In the first half of the eighteenth century a drift was perceptible in these population figures:

	1700	1750
City of London within the walls	139,300	87,000
City of London without the walls	69,000	57,300

The movement at that time was gradual. The population explosion was to come in the nineteenth century.

Year	City	County	Outer ring	Greater London
1801	128,129	831,181	155,334	1,114,644
1901	26,923	4,509,618	2,044,864	6,581,402

These nineteenth-century figures are reflected in widespread construction of bridges and tunnels crossing the tideway—almost completing the pattern which serves Greater London today. These works owed much technically to the new skills, equipment and materials of the Industrial Revolution, though bridge-building know-how had existed during those five and a half centuries and the spanning of the Thames with the use of available materials and labour presented no insuperable problems. While the old bridge was under repair, for instance, temporary wooden bridges had been built to serve the city. It is probable that Sir Christopher Wren would have occupied himself with a bridge at Blackfriars or Westminster if he had not been so taken up with the noble task of rebuilding St Paul's and the city churches and if the Great Fire of London had not diminished the financial resources of the city. Elements of civic pride, commercial chauvinism and obsession with tradition seem to have combined to give the solitary old bridge a monopoly. In 1722, for instance, when a bridge at Westminster was first proposed, a petition against it was presented to Parliament by the Company of Watermen, the West Country Bargemen, the Borough of Southwark, the City itself and also the inhabitants of old London Bridge. This, in spite of the fact that the considerable amount of traffic requiring a crossing west of the city had to rely upon the horse-ferry at Lambeth.

Thomas Pennant the naturalist (1726–98) left this note of the period: 'I well remember the street on London Bridge, narrow, darksome, and dangerous to passengers from the multitude of carriages: frequent arches of strong timber crossed the street, from the tops of the houses, to keep them together, and from falling into the river. Nothing but use could preserve the rest of the inmates, who soon grew deaf to the noise of the falling waters, the clamours of watermen, or the frequent shrieks of drowning wretches.'

In the year when they were all petitioning against a bridge at Westminster, the traffic on London Bridge was presenting such a problem that an order had to be issued by the Court of the Lord Mayor, the Aldermen and the Common Council for the appointing of three traffic controllers:

> This Court being sensible of the great inconveniences and Mischiefs by the disorderly Leading and Driving of Cars, Carts, Coaches and other Carriages, over London-Bridge, whereby the common Passage there is greatly obstructed, doth strictly order and injoin (pursuant to several former Orders made by this Court, for Prevention of those Mischiefs) That three sufficient and able Persons be appointed and constantly maintained; one by the Governors of Christ's Hospital, one by the Inhabitants of the Ward of Bridge Within, and the other by the Bridge-Masters: Which three persons are to give their diligent and daily Attendance at each End of the Bridge, and by all good Means to hinder and prevent the said Inconveniences; and for that purpose, to direct and take Care that all Carts, Coaches, and other Carriages coming out of Southwark into this City, do keep all along on the West Side of the said Bridge; (i.e. to the left) and all Carts, and Coaches, and other Carriages, going out of this City, do keep all along on the East Side of the said Bridge; and that no carman be suffered to stand a-cross the said Bridge, to load or to unload; and that they shall apprehend all such who shall be refractory, or offend herein, and carry them before some of his Majesty's Justices of the Peace for this City and Liberties, to be dealt with according to Law. And further, to prevent the aforesaid Obstructions, it is ordered, That the Collector of the Tolls upon the said Bridge shall take care that the said Duties be collected without making a Stay of the Carts, for which the same is to be paid.

There was to be no fumbling over the money; the traffic was to be kept moving. The tolls levied at that time were as follows:

For every cart or waggon with shod wheels	4*d*
For drays with five Barrrels	1*d*
For each pipe or butt	1*d*
For a ton of any goods	2*d*
For anything less than a ton	1*d*

Though there was a strong party in the Common Council in favour of pulling down the bridge during the eighteenth century, particularly after the advantages of the new Westminster Bridge were realized, the majority voted in favour of improving the structure. It was reported by the Common Council 'that the houses upon London Bridge are a public nuisance, long felt, and universally censured and complained of'. Accordingly between 1758 and 1762 the whole of the superstructures were demolished and the width of the thoroughfare was increased from 20 to 46 feet. To facilitate navigation the ninth pier from the south was removed so that a great central arch could be formed for shipping. The tolls for crossing over the bridge were increased. Strong objections were made to the tolls on vessels passing beneath the bridge. Though 'shooting' of the bridge cost an average loss of life of fifty bargees and watermen a year the improvements did not satisfy anybody as the flow of water through the great arch had been rendered even more dangerous by the existence of Westminster Bridge. The scale levied was as follows:

For every hoy, barge, vessel, lighter or other craft having any goods on board not exceeding five tons burthen, for every time any such craft shall pass through any of the arches of the Bridge, Two Pence.
Not exceeding ten tons, Threepence.
Not exceeding twenty-five tons, Sixpence.
And above the burthen of twenty-five tons, One shilling.

Exemptions were for craft loaded only with straw, manure, dung, compost or lime to be used for tillage.

While those concerned with navigation complained about the hazards and levies of the bridge those who passed over it had cause to complain of congestion. For a bridge which by this time was structurally unsound the traffic using it was prodigious. In one July day in 1811 the account of crossings of the bridge amounted to '89,640 persons on foot, 769 wagons, 2,924 carts and drays, 1,240 coaches, 485 gigs and taxed carts, and 764 horses'. It was not until a decade after this census that an Act was passed 'for rebuilding London Bridge, and for improving and making suitable approaches thereto'. The Corporation was then charged with the work of carrying this out. Premiums had already been offered for the best designs, with such reputable figures as Nash and Soane as judges. The acceptable design came from John Rennie the elder, who had just completed Waterloo Bridge. On his death in 1821 the work was undertaken by his son John. In a cavity in the bridge foundations, among various other items was placed a brass plate having an inscription composed in Latin and English by the Master of Oriel College, Oxford. It was a sad obituary, ignoring Peter de Colechurch, extolling George IV, but it shows the mood of the times.

> The free course of the river being obstructed by the numerous piers of the ancient bridge, and the passage of boats and vessels through its narrow channels being often attended with danger and loss of life by reason of the force and rapidity of the current, the City of London, desirous of providing a remedy for this evil, and at the same time consulting the convenience of commerce in this vast emporium of all nations, under the sanction and with the liberal aid of Parliament, resolved to erect a new bridge upon a foundation altogether new, with arches of a wider span, and of a character corresponding to the dignity and importance of this royal city: nor does any other time seem to be more suitable for such an undertaking than when, in a period of universal peace, the British Empire flourishing in glory, wealth, population, and domestic union, is governed by a prince, the patron and encourager of the arts, under whose auspices the metropolis has been daily advancing in elegance and splendour.

London had indeed advanced in elegance and splendour. Georgian and Regency architecture proliferated. The Rennies' London Bridge, for all its merits, was not a pioneering effort. To meet the needs of London's expansion other bridges had at last been planned and constructed toward the end of the eighteenth century. Before reviewing this first wave of bridge construction of which London Bridge was a part, it is as well to consider a human element which had throughout history been concerned with crossing the tideway—the Thames watermen, a skilled, vociferous and sometimes powerful section of the community whose members still man the waterway.

4

The Watermen

The river was the main thoroughfare of the nation and the men who served this waterway were important members of the community whose rights, skills and rewards had to be regulated from the earliest times. A Statute of Henry VIII dated 1514, for instance, stated 'that it had been a laudable custome and usage *tyme out of mind* to use the river in barge or whery bote', inferring rightly that the affairs of the Thames watermen and their craft went back before recorded history. The resplendence of the Royal Watermen reflected the importance attached to this calling. Before the introduction of coaches and roads fit for wheeled traffic, the palaces of the sovereigns lay by the river. The waterway was the only means of conveyance of the monarch between Windsor, Sheen, Hampton, Westminster, Whitehall, Bridewell, the Tower and Greenwich. The mobility of royalty and of government depended therefore upon a great retinue of skilled watermen. With only the solitary bridge at London for many centuries, a great and profitable burden rested upon the strong arms of oarsmen. From the reign of Elizabeth I until well on into the eighteenth century there were something like twenty thousand watermen engaged on or about the Thames tideway. Before Old London Bridge was built there was a ferry between Southwark and Churchyard Alley, near St Magnus the Martyr in the city. The rights in the ferry belonged to the city and they were rented by a waterman named John Overs. The rights were evidently hereditary for when he died he left them to his only daughter Mary. She sent word of her good fortune to her lover, who is not named in the story but who responded so eagerly to the news that in riding to London to join her he broke his neck. Mary Overs continued in charge of the profitable ferry and turned for consolation to good works. She founded a nunnery on the site of what was afterwards St Mary Overy's Church, where she was buried. After her death the nunnery was converted into a college for priests and it was this brotherhood which concerned itself with the upkeep and repair of the early timber bridges. It is likely that Peter de Colechurch himself was associated in some way with these good men and thus acquired his skills.

St Mary Overy's stairs, as the Southwark terminal of the ferry became known, were frequently used not only as a place for crossing as an alternative to the bridge, but as a place of embarkation for those passing through the bridge. It was from here that the Duke of Norfolk embarked on his barge on a dark November evening in 1428 with 'many a gentilman, squyer and yoman'. His watermen miscalculated the shooting of the bridge and the barge collided with one of the starlings 'whiche was cause of spyllyng of many a gentilman and othere, the more ruthe was'. The Duke himself with several of his companions managed to jump clear onto a starling as the vessel shot through, and he was duly rescued by ropes. The rest of his company and the vessel were carried through and 'overwhelmed'. The skills of the Thames watermen were traditionally taxed to the utmost in the shooting of the rapids of London Bridge and the casualties were high. The passage was never without some danger but at certain states of the tide it was almost lethal.

Cardinal Wolsey was one who avoided the shooting of the bridge. At the height of his power when he was residing in Whitehall keeping his own retinue of watermen, his downriver journeys to visit the King were described by Cavendish:

He used also every Sunday to resorte to the Courte, then being for the most parte of all the yeere at Greenwiche, with his former triumphs, taking his barge at his own stairs, furnished with yeomen, standing upon the bayles, and his gentlemen being within a boat, and landed again at the Three Cranes in the vintree, and from thence he rode upon his mule, with his crosses, his pillers, his hat, and the broad seal carried before him on horseback, through Thames street until he came to Billingsgate, and there took his barge againe, and so rowed to Greenwiche, where he was nobly received, &.

It became a well-established custom for the prudent or faint-hearted wishing to avoid the bridge to use the stairs at the Three Cranes, which was in the Vintrey in Upper Thames Street above the bridge, and the stairs at Billingsgate below the bridge. But there were watermen who made a speciality of the navigation of London Bridge and of course became known as bridge-shooters. These were celebrated by John Leland:

> Yet here we may not longer stay,
> But shoot the bridge and dart away,
> Though with restless fall, the tide
> Is dashing on the bulwarks' side;
> And roaring torrents drown my song
> As o'er the surge I drift along.

Samuel Pepys, who was so much on the water, was well aware of the hazards. In 1661 he wrote: 'Towards Westminster from the Tower, by water . . . and was fain to stand upon one of the piers [meaning the surface of a starling] about the bridge, before the men could drag their boat through the lock, and which they could not do until another was called to help them.' He also relates the story of a Frenchman's passage through the bridge: 'When he saw the great fall he began to cross himself and say his prayers in the greatest fear in the world, and soon as he was over, he swore, "Morbleu! c'est le plus grand plaisir du monde", being the most like a French humour in the world.'

Gordon Home culled a series of eighteenth-century newspaper items indicating how the hazards of the bridge at that time were almost taken for granted.

1758 Yesterday morning as a boat was coming thro' London bridge, with six passengers, it unluckily overset, but several boats putting off to their assistance, happily no person was lost.

1763 Yesterday as two Lightermen were striving one with the other to get the first through London Bridge, the Lighters struck one against the other, and both sank; one of them was loaded with Coals and the other with Stone. The Watermen were saved by Boats which instantly put off to their Assistance.

1763 Yesterday a Boat, with ten people in it, going through London-Bridge, in order to go down the river, overset, and three People were drowned; the others were taken up by some Boats which put off to their assistance.
On Tuesday Night a Barge, heavy loaded with Timber, coming through London-Bridge, ran against one of the Starlings, and carried Part of it away, and by the Shock John Herbert, one of the Bargemen, unfortunately, fell overboard and was drowned.

1767 On Monday night, a little before ten o'clock, a boat with three women and two men going through London-Bridge overset, and all perished. Several boats with links and lanthorns put off as soon as possible, but too late to save anyone.

1770 This morning as a boat was going through London Bridge it was overset, by which means two men lost their lives.

Samuel Johnson, another frequent user of the river, who relished taking part in the vituperation for which the watermen of his day were notorious, evidently made a habit of avoiding London Bridge. Boswell, describing their setting out for Greenwich, says: 'We landed at the "Old Swan", and walked to Billingsgate where we took oars and moved smoothly along silver Thames.'

The bridge-shooters were concerned principally with the main traffic up and down the river but there was a large body of watermen which plied across from stair to stair. At Gravesend a distinction was always made between the 'long ferry' which plied to and from the metropolis and the 'cross ferry' which has always run over to Tilbury. For centuries both ferries were of immense importance, the long ferry being one of London's main supply lines. The cross ferry, which still exists, diminished to the use of passengers only, connected Essex and the eastern counties not just with Kent but with the road which ran between Gravesend and the Channel ports and with the long ferry route to the metropolis. Putney served a similar purpose for the western approach to

London. Domesday Book states that the ferry there was estimated
to yield twenty shillings a year to the lord of the manor. '. . . the
place was a considerable thoroughfare', states Humpherus in his
account of the watermen, 'as it was usual for persons travelling to
the west of England to go as far as Putney by water.' Within the
metropolis, the Horseferry at Lambeth was the most popular
alternative to London Bridge.

From the time of the formation of the Company of Watermen
in 1555 (the Lightermen were embodied in the Company at the
beginning of the eighteenth century) there was ceaseless conflict
between the men of the river and the men of the roads. When the
Roman roads decayed, wheeled vehicles almost disappeared.
Except for the waterways, personal travel was on foot or on horseback and almost all other transport was by packhorses. In the
sixteenth century chariots were introduced in London for ceremonial occasions. Queen Mary Tudor rode in one drawn by six
horses to her coronation. Her successor, Queen Elizabeth, ordered
one for her retinue of ladies in April 1557 and this ornate affair
caused something of a revolution. Lilly, the dramatist, in 1584
wrote of those who used to go 'on hard-trotting horses, now riding
in easie coaches up and down to court ladies'. He follows with the
complaint that the streets of London were 'almost stopped up
with them'.

The watermen began protesting against this new traffic from
the sixteenth century onwards, sometimes pathetically, sometimes fiercely, as in due course the ferrymen were to protest
against the construction of bridges and tunnels whenever they
were initiated. John Taylor (1580–1653), the waterman poet,
wrote:

> Carroaches, coaches, jades, and Flanders mares,
> Doe rob us of our shares, our wares, our fares:
> Against the ground we stand and knocke our heeles,
> Whilest all our profit runs away on wheels:
> And whosoever but observes and notes,
> The great increase of coaches and of boates,
> Shall finde their number more than e'er they were
> By halfe and more within these thirty yeeres.
> Then watermen at sea had service still,
> And those that staid at home had worke at will;

Then upstart hellcart-coaches were to seeke,
A man could scare see twenty in a week,
But now I think a man may daily see,
More than the whirries on the Thames can be.

There was always a section of public opinion which maintained that the watermen abused their monopoly and brought many of their troubles upon themselves. Their conduct certainly came under official censure in an Act of Parliament in 1603 concerning Wherrymen and Watermen. This provided that apprentices under eighteen years of age were not to be allowed to carry passengers and the reason given was that 'It hath often happened that divers and sundry people passing by water upon the River of Thames between Windsor and Gravesend have been put to great hazard and danger and the loss of their lives and goods, and many times have perished and been drowned in the said River through the unskilfulness and want of knowledge or experience in the wherrymen and watermen.'

The Thames watermen were also notorious for what was known as 'water language'. This was spiced with oaths, vituperation and abuse and it often took the form of topical ribaldry. From the Middle Ages the water language became almost a privileged tradition similar to that of court jesters, and royal passengers did not escape the gibes. Indeed it has been suggested that the commissioning of Handel to compose the Water Music for a progress of the first of the Hanoverian kings upon the tideway was in fact partly an effort to drown a volley of water language which might well have been misunderstood by that monarch.

A portrait of the poet John Taylor hangs in a place of honour in the Watermen's Hall at St Mary-at-Hill, for Taylor left ample records of his extraordinary life. He was born at Gloucester, where he was at grammar school, and on being ploughed in his Latin exams, came to the metropolis to be apprenticed to a London waterman. He was pressed into the Navy, like so many of his brethren who for centuries were the constant victims of press-gangs. After the siege of Cadiz in 1596 he returned to become a waterman with rhyming as a sideline. He enjoyed a considerable success with the patronage of Ben Jonson, arranged water pageants and composed triumphs for the pageants of Lord Mayors. He was nothing if not a showman. In 1619, for instance, he set out from London to Queenborough in a brown paper boat and narrowly escaped drowning. After taking refuge at Oxford to escape the Plague he published in 1630 'All the Workes of John Taylor, the Water Poet'. His fulminations against coach traffic met with some success. Through the Watermen's Company he was able to bring about a restriction of carriages in London. For some thirty-five years they were banned unless their journeys ended at least two miles from the river.

He was at his best in a pamphlet published in 1613 called 'The Cause of the Watermen's Suit Concerning Players'. This was the golden age of the theatres, such as Shakespeare's Globe on the south bank, no playhouses being permitted within the metropolis. With James I on the throne there seemed some likelihood that the playhouse might be allowed to move across the river, which would have been disastrous for the ferrymen since most of London went to the theatre by water. The watermen had already fallen on hard times and this new threat to their livelihood engaged the whole eloquence of the poet who was universally regarded as their spokesman.

> I must confess that there are many rude uncivil fellows in our Company, and I would some doctor would purge the Thames of them: the reason whereof is, that all men being vicious, by consequence most vice must be in the greatest Companies, but watermen are the greatest Company, therefore most abuses must reign amongst watermen; yet, (not to excuse them in any degree) let a man but consider other trades and faculties of higher account, and I am sure they will come short in honesty, perhaps not of watermen, but of the honest vocation of a waterman.
>
> For he use no labour otherwise than he ought, which is to carry the King's liege people carefully, and to land them safely, to take his due thankfully without murmuring or doing injury, then I say, that that waterman may feed upon the labours of his hands with a better conscience, and sleep with a quieter spirit than many of our fur gowned money-mongers that are accounted good commonwealths men; but if a railing knave do chance to abuse his fare, either in words or deeds, (as indeed we have too many such) what reason is it, that for the wrong that one, two, or more doth commit, that all the rest of the whole Company shall be scandalized for it. . . .

I have seen a usurer (who hath been fit only for the grave these seven years being more than half rotten with the gout, the cough, and the mur) who hath lost his conscience to get money, and perhaps, win damnation, who is not able to go by land, and yet will not pay his fare by water, but like the picture of misery, will either beg his passage of some serving man, or bargain with a waterman to give him two pence for six pennyworth of labour, such I have seen, and such there are too many, who if they were once buried, the wheel of time would turn, and what they got unjustly by extortion, oppression, and grinding the faces of the poor, what they have uncharitably pinched in keeping back the labourer's hire, their sons or heirs perhaps will consume in law who shall possess most of that ill gotten goods, or else drink it, dice it, drab it, revel and ruffle it, till all is gone . . .

I myself have often met with a roaring boy (or one of the cursed crew) that hath nothing about him but a satin outside to cover his knavery, and that none of his own neither, witness his mercer and his tailor: yet this gallant must be shipped in a pair of oars at least: but his gay slop hath no sooner kissed the cusions, but with a volley of new coined oaths . . . he hath never left roaring, row, row, row, a pox on you row . . . and when his scurviness is landed where he pleases, he hath told me I must wait on him, and he will return to me presently, and I shall carry him back again, and be paid altogether: then have I attended five or six hours (like John-a-Noakes) for nothing, for my cheating shark having neither money nor honesty, hath never come at me, but took someother pair of Stairs, and in the same fashion cozened another waterman for his boat-hire. . . .

And as before I have written, our trade is so useful and necessary both for the King's service and the commons commodity, that it is not to be (or cannot be wanted) and by how much the more a waterman is near to his Majesty, to the Queen's Majesty, to the Princess Highness, to the nobility, the gentry, and the best of the commonalty of this kingdom, and sometimes of foreign nations, so much the more ought watermen to behave themselves honestly, and soberly in their calling: There are many better trades and qualities, that scarce the best of their Companies in all their life time do come so often and so near the presence of Majesty and Nobility as we do. (I write not to disparage any, nor with boasting to puff up ourselves) none comes nearer, except the barber, and long and often may he come, or the physician and chirurgeon, (which God grant they may be ever needless:) but a waterman many times has his Sovereign by the hand, to stay him in and out the barge, where there is not above an inch betwixt life and death, the barge being then the Royal Court: and being but a door

betwixt the King and them, they are at that time gentlemen of the
privy chamber, or yeomen of the guard at least.

The waterman's pride in his calling was justified, for to work a
ferry throughout the year at all states of weather and tide when the
only alternative to a ferry was but a single bridge called for skill,
strength and experience. From 1603 to 1827 a seven-year
apprenticeship had to be served by every waterman. Since 1827 the
apprenticeship has been for five, six or seven years. It has started
between the ages of fourteen and twenty in order that the boy
should not come out of his time until the age of twenty-one. In
spite of the virtual disappearance of ferries and the mechanization
of so much of the work on the tideway the Watermen's Company,
which still conducts under Act of Parliament the enrolment of
apprenticeships and the examination for watermen's licences, is,
in the seventies of this century, dealing with an intake of fifteen to
twenty apprentices every year. For any waterman plying for hire
to carry fare-paying passengers must hold a licence from the
Waterman's Company, which they have granted continually
since 1555 and which they now issue on behalf of the Port of
London Authority.

From such writings as John Taylor's it might have been
assumed that the work of the ferrymen of his period would have
been safeguarded as an essential service, yet because of their
nautical skills they were in constant danger of impressment for the
Navy, and year after year pleas went out for their relief. At the
end of the Dutch War in 1668, for instance, according to the
records of the Watermen's Company '. . . considerable difficulty
arose as to many of the apprentices obtaining their freedom of the
company, in consequence of their masters having been killed when
serving in the royal navy. . . .' The following is typical of a petition
to Charles II to alleviate the distress in a single case:

> To the King's most excellent Majesty.
> The humble peticon of Robert Drewitt, Waterman, sheweth,
> That your petitioner hath voluntarily and faithfully served your
> sacred Majestie at sea, under ye command of Capt. Shepheard,
> Capt. Breeman, and Capt. Fosby, as they can and will testifie, yet
> upon some misinformacon your petitioner is disfranchised and
> deprived of ye privileges of his freedom, to ye utter ruine of your

petitioner his wife and family, unless relieved by your sacred Majestie; for although ye masters of ye Companie of Watermen to whom your petitioner hath applyed himself are very senceable of ye greate injury done him, yet know not how to right him without your Majestie's pleasure be signified therein.

May it therefore please your sacred Majestie graciously to vouchsafe him your order to ye masters of ye said company to restore him to his freedom, he having, as in duty bound, ever been and shall be ready to adventure his life and fortunes to ye utmost for your sacred Majesty.

This was the royal answer:

His Majesty in consideration of ye petitioner's service done ye late warrs at sea, is graciously pleased to refer the peticoner to ye masters of ye Company of Watermen, to allow the peticoners freedom of ye said company, with such priviledges as they doe others that have served their time to ye same trade.

It was the liability of watermen for impressment which inspired Dibdin to write his famous song

> Then farewell my trim-built wherry,
> Oars and coat, and badge farewell!
> Never more at Chelsea Ferry
> Shall your Thomas take a spell.
>
> But to hope and peace a stranger,
> In the battle's heat I'll go,
> Where exposed to every danger,
> Some friendly ball may lay me low.
>
> Then, mayhap, when homeward steering,
> With the news my messmates come,
> Even you my story hearing,
> With a sigh may cry 'poor Tom'.

This ferry in Chelsea Reach required considerable skill for there was an old saying among watermen 'that a set of fiddlers had been drowned in the Reach many years ago, and that the river had been occasionally dancing there ever since'. The ferry was an ancient one and presumably belonged to the Crown, for when James I came to the throne he granted for the sum of £40 to 'his dear relation, Thomas Earl of Lincoln, John Eldred, and Robert Henley, Esquires, all that ferry across the River Thames called Chelchehith ferry or Chelsey ferry'.

Such ferries were viable properties and in 1618 the Earl sold it to William Blake who owned Chelsea Park, who re-sold it two years later to the Earl of Middlesex. The frequency with which the ownership of the ferry changed hands was remarkable. In 1695 it belonged to Bartholomew Nutt, from whom it was acquired by Sir Walter St John, who owned the manor of Battersea and left it to his son, who died in 1742, being succeeded by his son Henry, Viscount Bolingbroke, who bequeathed it to his nephew in 1762, who obtained an Act of Parliament under which he sold it to the trustees of John, Earl Spencer.

When in 1726 a bridge had been proposed at Putney—and subsequently became the first of the eighteenth-century bridges on the tideway—the Chelsea ferryman put in a petition for compensation for loss of business. Because of the distance between the ferry and the new bridge the petition was thrown out.

Chelsea ferry is characteristic of many of the ancient ferries on the tideway. The owner, who had obtained his rights by grant, acquisition or inheritance, was in the position of a landlord and the ferryman's status was that of a tenant, though in many cases he could pass on his rights to an heir or a purchaser so long as his successor was a waterman.

The history of most of the ferries is singularly disputatious. There were conflicts between the owners and operators, and between rival ferry enterprises: but the main struggle, in which ferry owners and ferry operators joined forces, was against all improvements in transportation. It was a losing battle. With international trade in the port and industrial growth on land went the demand for more sophisticated transportation. The waterman protested in vain against the return of the wheel and the proliferation of vehicular transport in Tudor and Stuart times. Theirs was not a strong enough vested interest to stand against the building of bridges but by and large they delayed bridge construction: and when the first bridges were built they put in successful claims for compensation.

But some ferry owners transferred their interests into the construction or operation of bridges. For instance at Chelsea and at Battersea across the river, the population had increased in size and in sophistication by the middle of the eighteenth century. In 1766 a petition was presented to the House of Commons from the inhabitants of the neighbourhood, stating that the ferry was inconvenient and dangerous in bad weather and demanding a bridge. It was no coincidence that Earl Spencer, the owner of the ferry, submitted a separate petition at the same time stating that he was willing to build a bridge at his own expense upon having a reasonable toll granted—and this was what he did. The Bill was passed but it seemed that those who drew it had some doubts about the solidity of the work contemplated by the Earl. Special powers were granted to sue watermen who might injure the bridge 'by boat or vessel'. In the event of a tempest or unforeseen accident rendering the bridge dangerous or impracticable the Earl was to provide a 'convenient ferry, charging the same toll of one half-penny as on the bridge'.

5

Ferries and Ferrymen

The ferries to the east of the Tower of London, where bridge-building has not been practicable, were always important and have remained so until the present century, when their loads have been eased by the opening of tunnels. The Tilbury and Gravesend cross-ferry, which went out of service for vehicles when the Dartford tunnel was opened in the sixties, has such ancient origins that they are lost in history. In the earliest times it was a useful connection between Essex and Kent and a kind of feeder service for the long ferry. With the building of Tilbury Fort it became more valuable and it was then owned by the lords of the manors of Tilbury and Parrock. At the time of the Spanish Armada it was temporarily supplemented. In 1558 a bridge of boats was constructed between Tilbury and Gravesend as a means of communication for the army encamped at Tilbury Fort. Queen Elizabeth arrived in her barge and inspected the army and navy on both sides of the river. When the fleet sailed the temporary bridge was dismantled.

There was another occasion mentioned in the Watermen's records when a bridge of boats was laid out. This was in 1642, between Fulham and Putney, during the Civil War. In that year the Commander of Tilbury Fort, Captain John Talbot, in a petition to Charles I made a reference to the Gravesend ferry, the access to which curiously lay through the Fort. 'Moreover there is a ferry house and a ferry kept within the fort, by the lord of the soil, to his own benefit, through which passengers, with their cattle and commodities, (as through a common road and high-way) do pass from Essex unto Kent.'

Charles I had good reason to recall the existence of the ferry. In 1623 as Prince of Wales he and the Duke of Buckingham had occasion to cross incognito on their way to woo the Infanta of Spain. They lacked small change. When Buckingham gave the ferryman a gold piece the ungrateful fellow took them to be spies and had them arrested.

In 1694 Gravesend Corporation, a wealthy and influential body, purchased the manor of Parrock and thus acquired the Kent end of the ferry. The Governor of Tilbury Fort seized this opportunity to make an offer to forgo a considerable sum of back-pay which he was owed by the Army authorities in return for the right to operate the Essex end of the ferry and to build a public house for the convenience of passengers and 'for his ferrymen to dwell on the spot'. He succeeded in this and built the pub called the World's End, which remains to this day.

The ferrymen of Gravesend and Tilbury were the first to be threatened by under-Thames tunnel proposals. In 1798 an attempt, ill-conceived and ahead of its time, was actually made to sink shafts for a tunnel between Essex and Kent. More about this will be found in Chapter 9, pp. 91–5. It is only relevant to note here that an award was worked out in advance for compensation for loss of ferry rights. If the construction had gone through the tunnel company was to pay £110 a year.

With the advent of steam a company was formed in 1834 to supersede the wherries by using a floating bridge on chains to take horses, vehicles and passengers across the river. When the weight of the vessels and the strength of the tides made this difficult to work it was replaced by a steam tug which ran every fifteen minutes.

By the middle of the century, the division of ownership caused conflict—and appalling inefficiency. The south-bound ferry—that from Tilbury to Gravesend—was owned by the Government, represented by the Board of Ordnance. The north-bound ferry was owned by Gravesend Corporation. After much bickering the

Corporation took over the Board's interest in 1850 at a rental of
£50 per year for ninety-nine years. They then leased the rights of
the ferry in both directions to William Tisdall, who did not
improve matters. In 1854 there were complaints from the Army
that the ferry had gone from bad to worse and there was a threat
to terminate the Corporation's lease. The matter was resolved by
the approach of the London Tilbury and Southend Railway and
the emergence of the famous railroad pioneering names of Messrs
Peto, Betts and Brassey, who took over the ferry rights. Having
extended its railway tracks to the north shore, the railway company
was intent on tapping business south of the river by using the
ferry. Their first ferry steamer was an iron paddler called *Tilbury*,
later renamed *Sir Walter Raleigh*. It was later joined by the *Queen
Elizabeth*, the *Earl of Leicester* and the *Earl of Essex* (the last of
which rolled terribly).

When the Midland Railway took over the L.T.S.R. it also
acquired the ferry, introducing workmen's season tickets in 1914.
After nationalization British Railways ran a ferry service for
passengers and vehicles until the opening of the Dartford Tunnel,
when they obtained Parliamentary permission to end their legal
obligation to produce a vehicle ferry. In 1962 diesel vessels
replaced steam and this ancient ferry continued to be operated as
it has always been by Thames watermen.

The other important tideway ferry, which still operates at
Woolwich, may well owe its origin to an early ecclesiastical parish
grouping by which Lesnes Abbey, founded at Erith in 1178, was
granted or appropriated parishes and manors on the other side of
the Thames in Essex. The people of Woolwich, in those times a
small fishing village, possessed a right to run a ferry for which the
abbey received dues. An early reference to it appears in the state
papers in 1308, when the ferryman William de Wicton sold his
business to a mason called William Atte Halle for £10. There are
two references to its changing hands during that century. That it
became valuable not only financially but as a service was demon-
strated in 1330 when the people of Woolwich petitioned Parliament to suppress rival ferries at Greenwich and Erith because
theirs was a 'Royal ferry, favoured of the King'.

This is an early example of the ferryman's traditional right of action against any disturbance of his franchise or any diminishment of his custom by the setting up of any new crossing of the river whether it was by bridge, tunnel or ferry. In guarding his rights the ferryman sometimes carried public opinion with him, where the threat to his ferry was also a threat to local trade or amenities: more often in latter years he was fighting a lone battle against progress.

As Woolwich grew from a fishing village to a royal dockyard under the Tudors and the ordnance depot established there in the reign of Henry VIII became the Royal Arsenal, the ferry became increasingly important strategically as well as commercially.

In 1810 the Army established its own ferry, which ran between the Arsenal and the Old Barge House Landing Stage on the north bank. The following year saw the promotion of the Woolwich Ferry Company, whose shareholders included the lady of the manor, Dame Jane Wilson and her son, Sir Thomas Maryon Wilson. They obtained an Act of Parliament for 'a common ferry, consisting of one or more boats, or such other vessels as shall be sufficient and proper for the passage and conveyance of persons carriages, cattle, goods, wares and merchandise over the said River Thames. . . .' This was half a mile west of the town and the promoters claimed that it would not prejudice the trade of the inhabitants or of the watermen. The Act, however, imposed a penalty on anyone ferrying people or vehicles within half a mile of the ferry. The distance was increased to two miles by an amendmnet in 1815. The watermen through the Watermen's Company protested and succeeded in modifying the Act though in fact the western ferry continued to run until 1844 when the Company was dissolved, thousands of pounds having been lost. No dividend was ever distributed and no mention was ever made in the accounts of revenue derived from the working of the ferry.

'By 1828,' writes F. M. Fuller, 'the ferry seems to have been the sole concern of the landlord of *The Prince Regent*, who held his house at a rental which included the ferry service but which allowed him to retain all tolls. Charlton or West Woolwich pier was later built on the south bank site by a combination of watermen who settled in Trinity Street [now Warspite Road]—but it was later sold with all the ferry rights to a Mr. W. P. Jackson.'

Meanwhile the established Barge House Ferry prospered. Reporting in 1839 'the lessees of Woolwich ferry have within the last few weeks stationed here a new ferry boat of larger dimensions than any on the river, with a view to meeting the increase of traffic that has lately taken place between the two counties. Mr How, the proprietor of *The Old Barge House*, is constructing an esplanade extending along the banks of the river, 300 yards, the depth upwards of 130.'

Toward the middle of the nineteenth century the railways began to interest themselves in this crossing as they did at Gravesend. The Great Eastern Railway Company came to North Woolwich in 1846, and the following year began operating a ferry service with Barking-built steamers running in connection with the London trains. This venture was called 'The Eastern Counties Ferry' but was known by all who used it as the 'Penny Ferry'.

By the 1880s the crossings of the river between north and south Woolwich became a matter of public concern. A deputation of sixty townsfolk waited on the local Board to demand the establishment of a free steam ferry. They had a good case. Woolwich rates had contributed toward the abolition of tolls upon bridges in the prosperous western part of London. As we shall see later the Metropolitan Board of Works conceded the free ferry, which was inaugurated in 1889. This, with the foot tunnel which was eventually built to supplement it, will be dealt with in more detail in a later chapter (see pp. 145–8).

The coming of the first steam ferries to Woolwich, manned of course by watermen, did not immediately supersede the watermen who plied their oars. The hazards of ice and storm are frequently mentioned in the watermen's annals from the Middle Ages to the eighteenth century. Mist and fog are rarely mentioned. No doubt the Industrial Revolution contributed greatly to the hazards of the tideway. By 1873 Woolwich was industrialized and a multitude of workpeople had to be ferried every day between north and south Woolwich. On 25th October that year the river was fog-bound and the ferry steamer services were cancelled. In Woolwich in the early morning workmen gathered anxiously, hoping that the steam ferries might operate, reluctant to return home and lose a day's pay. When the cry went up 'Anyone for North Woolwich—

twopence a time' some of the men were prepared to trust them-
selves to the skill of the small boats and the local ferrymen, who
were licensed to carry eight persons in their craft. One of these,
Isaac Digby, took on a load, more than he should, at Bell Water
Gate. His passengers included John Wright, who worked in North
Woolwich; Thomas Smith, aged 65, a storekeeper at Silvertown;
Patrick Lanna aged 16; and John Taylor aged 15.

At 5.15 a.m. Digby pushed off and headed upstream before
striking out across the river, as there was a strong spring tide
flowing and he hoped to use this to drop down against the cause-
way at North Woolwich. The passengers, young and old, huddled
together apprehensively as the little boat moved silently into the
density of black fog. It was John Wright who spotted a glimmer
of light from a vessel at anchor and called out: 'It's all right,
thank God. We're safe! It's the ferry boat at North Woolwich.'

The lights in fact were those of the *Princess Alice* (later herself
the victim of a terrible disaster), moored at the Woolwich landing
stage from which the party had set out. The overloaded ferry had
not crossed the river but had been carried downstream. Within
a few seconds Digby's craft was swept down onto the steamer and
sucked under it. Digby himself, who was an experienced swimmer
and knew how to go with the tide, managed to struggle ashore.
John Wright hung onto the capsized ferry boat until he could
grasp the steamer's paddle box and save himself. The others were
lost.

Such watermen as Digby, prepared to risk their own lives and
the lives of others, were familiar to Charles Dickens and other
nineteenth-century writers who admired their skill and pride in
their craft and recognized that, as oarsmen at least, they were
following a dying occupation. Members of the Watermen's Company are still active on the tideway today as passenger carriers,
bargemen and lightermen but, except for relatively few pleasure
craft, the oarsmen have faded away. Henry Mayhew writing in
the 1860s reported a situation of decline: 'The present number of
Thames watermen (privileged and unprivileged) is, I am informed
by an officer of the Watermen's Hall, about 1,600. The Occupation Abstract of 1841 gives the number of London boat, barge,
and watermen as 1,654. The men themselves have very loose

notions as to their number. One man computed it to me at 12,000;
another at 14,000. This is evidently a traditional computation,
handed down from the days when watermen were in greater
requisition.'

In Mayhew's time the present pattern of bridges had already
emerged but still the great change which came over the tideway
with the demolition of Old London Bridge was a potent memory
for the watermen. Mayhew reported: '"It's neight this nor that,"
said an old waterman to me, alluding to the decrease in their
number and their earnings, "people may talk as they like about
what's been the ruin of us—it's nothing but new London Bridge.
When my old father heard that the old bridge was to come down,
Bill, says he, *it'll be up with the watermen in no time*. If the old bridge
had stood, how would all these steamers have shot her? Some of
them could never have got through at all. At some tides, it was so
hard to shoot London Bridge (to go clear through the arches),
that people wouldn't trust themselves to any but watermen. Now
any fool might manage. London Bridge, sir, depend on it, has
ruined us."'

But while Old London Bridge still stood and there were a
hundred stairs used by ferrymen in the metropolitan area, their
views and their wellbeing carried much weight. There is no
record of their having gone on strike, which might well have
caused chaos in the seventeenth or eighteenth century, but their
regulation and management and the constancy with which they
were impressed for service in the Navy had a direct effect on the
day-to-day life of the metropolis.

There was for instance the pious restrictive practice concerning
Sunday. In 1641 a Bill was passed restraining watermen from
working on the Lord's Day. This seems to have created a Sunday
black market for those wishing to cross the river, and the Watermen's Company had to devise some service for the public which
would not infringe the religious scruples of the period. This took
the form of an Act passed in 1700 which recited:

> that great numbers of idle and loose boys do work on the Lord's
> day, commonly called Sunday, and exact large prices from
> passengers whose necessary occasions oblige them to pass and
> repass the river of Thames, and generally spend such their gains

in drunkenness and profaneness the succeeding week, and that for
prevention thereof, and to the end that what shall be got thereby,
might be applied to the charitable relief of such aged and
maimed watermen and lightermen, their widows and children,
whose circumstances wanted assistance [it was enacted] that
it should be lawful for the rulers, overseers, auditors and
assistants of the company on their court days, to appoint any number of watermen not exceeding forty, to ply and work on every
Lord's day between Vauxhall and Limehouse, at such common
stairs or places of plying, as to the court should seem convenient,
for carrying and re-carrying persons across the river at one penny
each; such watermen on every Monday paying over to the court
the sums received by them, and such court paying such men for
their day's labour, and the overplus should from time to time be
applied to the use of the poor, aged, decayed and maimed watermen, lightermen and their widows.

A year or so later when there were still disputes about the
running of the Sunday ferries and who should run them, the
Attorney-General made the following statement: 'I am of opinion
the intent of this act was to provide for the necessary passage of
persons over the river on Sundays and to dispense with the statute
for the better observation of the Lord's day, by which act watermen were restrained from rowing on Sundays, and by this act the
company are weekly to appoint the forty that are to work on
Sunday, but they cannot make a farm of it; but having appointed
them, they are on every Monday morning to take the account of
the money received by them on Sunday, and allowing each of
them for their day's work, are to receive the rest of what they
shall gain, and apply it to the use of such poor of the said society
as the act directs, and this is all they can do.'

It seems that the watermen themselves were responsible for
carrying out such regulations and those who took their weekly
turn at the 'suppressing of all manner of offenders' have their
names duly noted in the records at Watermen's Hall.

Mention of poor watermen, distressed watermen's families and
funds and charities provided to relieve them occurs frequently in
the records, from the Middle Ages until Victorian times. This
insecurity and vulnerability in the watermen's calling was partly
due to natural causes and partly to the defence needs of the times.
The waterman was the victim of his own skill, a ready-made

sailor conveniently placed for impressment aboard the naval
vessels, so many of which were built at Deptford and Woolwich.
As we have seen, watermen frequently appealed against the
activities of the press gangs and obtained a fair measure of relief,
but most of them at some time or other saw service in the Navy—
John Taylor, the water poet, was pressed seven times—and that
meant that they suffered heavy casualties and the Watermen's
Company was called upon to look after a great many disabled men
and naval widows. Apart from this liability, Nature offered considerable occupational risks, and the ferrymen were navigating
small frail craft on a strongly tidal waterway which was frequently
crowded. Just as the London of the Middle Ages, the Tudors and
the Stuarts was vulnerable to fire and storm, so were the craft,
frail by modern standards, that plied for hire and used the tideway vulnerable to the storms and tempests which were not infre-
quently recorded. In November 1703, for instance, Humpherus
records a storm of wind continuing for several days.

> It was strange to find all the ships blown away, the pool was so
> clear, not above four ships left between Wapping and Ratcliff
> Cross; some had nobody on board, a great many but a man and
> boy; there was nothing to be done but to let them drive how they
> would, which they did one into another, and laid them so upon
> one another as it were in heaps. There laid near seven hundred
> sail of ships between Shadwell and Limehouse all adrift and
> driving over one another, several sunk. Those who viewed the
> place and posture of the vessels, imagined their situation impos-
> sible to describe. Five ships bound for the West Indies, went on
> shore near Tilbury fort, but got off afterwards luckily in conse-
> quence of a very high tide following the storm, so that people were
> compelled to take boats to get to Westminster Hall. The water-
> men reckoned above five hundred wherries lost, most of which
> were not sunk only, but dashed to pieces against each other or
> against the ships and shore where they lay; ships and boats with-
> out number were driven about in every corner, sunk and staved,
> and about three hundred men were supposed to be lost. Abun-
> dance of lighters and barges drove quite through the bridge and
> took their fate below, whereof many were lost; above sixty barges
> and lighters were afterwards found driven foul of the bridge,
> which was entirely blocked up, and sixty more sunk or staved,
> between the bridge and Hammersmith. It was impossible to tell
> the number of deaths on the river. Twelve men of war were lost

on the coast, &c., and upwards of eighteen thousand men perished, besides the loss of a great number of merchant ships.

Even more than storm and tempest the enemy of the watermen was ice. Between the thirteenth and the eighteenth centuries records show the tideway to have been obstructed or completely frozen over to an extent unknown in this century. This was probably due to the river being less embanked as well as to the winter climate being more severe, and to some extent to the barrage effect of Old London Bridge. In the Watermen's records the severe frosts totally blocking the river are mentioned four times in the thirteenth century, three times in the fifteenth century, when in 1408 the freeze-up continued for fourteen weeks, and four times in the sixteenth century, when in 1537 King Henry VIII with Jane Seymour and the court 'crossed the river on the ice to Greenwich Palace on horseback'. In the seventeenth century the river was very frequently frozen over and frost fairs came into their own. In 1684 a great frost lasted for many weeks, during which printing presses operated on the frozen river and large boats were used as sledges 'some of them being drawn by horses and others by watermen in want of their usual employment'.

These were bad times indeed for the ferrymen.

At this time [writes Humpherus] there was a foot passage quite over the river, from Lambeth stairs to the Horseferry, at Westminster, and Hackney coaches began to carry fares from Somerset House and the Temple to Southwark. On January twenty-third, the first day of Hilary Term, they were regularly employed in hire where the watermen were accustomed to be found. . . .

Was the winter climate of the eighteenth century particularly severe or were the records of freezing conditions more meticulously kept? In the annals of Watermen's Hall, which were not so much concerned with the affairs of the nation or the metropolis as with those who worked on the river, there are as many as twenty references in that century to the watermen being put out of business by severe and prolonged frost.

When the river was entirely frozen over during the winter of

1762–3, distress among watermen was such that public subscriptions were raised.

> During its continuance, [writes Humpherus,] a party of watermen with a wherry on their shoulders and one of their number sitting in the same with oars, began collecting money from charitable people to relieve their families. Large sums were given by the public to relieve the general distress, His Majesty contributing one thousand pounds for that purpose; many persons were found frozen to death both on land and the water; at Gravesend, all work upon the river was stopped, the intercourse with London by water suspended, and the Rochester and Gravesend tide coaches which ran to and from the tide boats at Gravesend, commenced running up to London.

No wonder one of the popular broadsides of the period entitled 'The Thames encased, or, the Watermen's Song upon the Thaw', began with the words:

> Come ye merry men all
> Of Watermen's Hall,
> Let's hoist out our boats and caressing;
> The Thames it does melt,
> And the cold is scarce felt,
> Not an icicle is now to be seen.

In this century there has been at least one famous occasion when a waterman stood out for his ferrying rights and not even the tumult of the First World War prevented him from being seen as something of a democratic hero. The man was Walter Hammerton of Eel Pie Island, his antagonist was William John Manners, Earl of Dysart, the dates of their encounter were 1909–15, and the place was Twickenham Ferry, celebrated in the song:

> Ahoy! and Oho, and it's who's for the ferry?
> (The briar's in bud and the sun going down:)
> And I'll row ye so quick and I'll row ye so steady,
> And tis but a penny to Twickenham Town. . . .

Contrary to general belief this is not a traditional ditty. The writer of the words, Theophile Julius Henry Marzials, was in fact alive when the Earl clashed with the waterman on the ferry rights, though he added no topical lines to his verses. He died in 1920.

Lord Dysart, who lived at Ham House, owned by inheritance the ferry between Twickenham and Ham. The Hammerton family were watermen, boatbuilders and hirers and bargemen who started a ferry at some distance downstream from the existing one to serve people crossing from Richmond to Marble Hill, at that time newly opened as a public park. In 1909 Lord Dysart served a writ on Walter Hammerton claiming that his ferry was an infringement of the Earl's rights. This was followed in 1910 by an offer from the Earl to Hammerton to work the ferry in his service at a yearly rental. Hammerton refused: 'if I had accepted this licence' he afterwards reported to the *Richmond and Twickenham Times*, 'I should have jeopardised the public rights for my own benefit.' Dysart then went to law, claiming that his ferry rights were not merely from one particular point to another but from any part of Twickenham to any part of Ham or Petersham. Hammerton won the first round in April 1913. The Earl appealed and his appeal was upheld. Hammerton then proposed to carry the fight to the House of Lords. Local residents in the year the First World War broke out then formed a Thames Rights Protection Committee to support Hammerton. The war was already a year old when in 1915 Hammerton won and a celebration regatta was held. A commemoration song was composed entitled 'The Ferry to Fairyland', the profits from it being donated to the Waterman's Almshouses Benevolent Fund. The hero of the day, Walter Hammerton, already a freeman of the Thames, was made a freeman of the City of London.

6

A Start on Bridges

Old London Bridge was to be the only crossing ever to contain an element of piety and to arouse intense feelings of pride. Though bridge-building may surely be rated a noble, or at least benign, occupation in itself, the proposals for the first bridges to relieve the burdens borne solely by London Bridge for five centuries were attended by debates in which public need was only just able to make its way against every kind of pressure from vested interest and prejudice. The report of a Commons debate rejecting an early proposal for a bridge at Putney in 1671 offers some insight into the attitudes which kept London west of the old bridge bridgeless for such an inordinately long time.

Mr JONES (Member for London).—This Bill will question the very being of London; next to the pulling down of the Borough of Southwark, nothing can ruin it more. All the correspondences westward for fuel, and grain, and hay, if this bridge be built cannot be kept up. The water there is shallow at ebb; the correspondences of London require free passage at all times, and if a bridge, a sculler can scarce pass at low water; it will alter the affairs of watermen to the King's damage, and the nation's.— Thinks the Bill unreasonable and unjust.

Mr WALLER (the Poet).—As for the imposition laid by this Bill, men may go by water if they please and not over the bridge; and so pay nothing. If ill for Southwark, it is good for this end of the town where Court and Parliament are. At Paris there are many bridges,—at Venice, hundreds,—we are still obstructing public things. The King cannot hunt, but he must cross the water. He, and the whole Nation have convenience by it.

Sir THOMAS LEE.—This Bill will make the new buildings at this end of the Town let the better, and fears the Bill is only for that purpose.

COLONEL BIRCH.—Finds it equal to men, whether it does them hurt, or they think it does them hurt. Where a cart carries something to the City, it usually brings something home; and they that bring provision hither, will fetch back, but will not go to the City to fetch it.

Mr Secretary TREVOR.—No law can be made but will transfer one or other inconvenience somewhere, passages over rivers are generally convenient; and by the same reason you argue against this bridge, you may argue against London Bridge and the ferries.

Sir WILLIAM THOMPSON.—When a convenience has been so long possessed as this has been, it is hard to remove it. This will make the skirts (though not London) too big for the whole body; the rents of London Bridge, for the maintenance of it will be destroyed. This bridge will cause sands and shelves, and have an effect upon the low bridge navigation, and cause the ships to lie as low as Woolwich; it will affect your navigation, your seamen, and your western barges who cannot pass at low water,—would reject the Bill.

COLONEL STROUDE.—In no city where bridges are, they were all built at a time. No city in the world is so long as ours, and here is but one passage for five miles.—In frosts provisions may stop, and in case of any mutiny passages may be so stopped by water; as a correspondence cannot be held any way but by this convenience.

Mr BOSCAWEN.—If a bridge at Putney, why not at Lambeth, and more? And as for Paris where there are many bridges, there is no use for watermen at all: and the same reason that serves Paris may serve London; neither Middlesex nor Surrey desire it, at best it is but a new conclusion.

Sir JOHN BENNETT.—Says the Lord Mayor and Aldermen did agree to it, if it were for no other reason than to be secured from a bridge at Lambeth.

Mr. LOVE.—The Lord Mayor of this year is of a different opinion from him of the last year; if carts go over, the City must be destroyed by it. It is said that it encourages but a few ferrymen, though in truth it does many.—He hears that it must be of timber, which must be vast; and will so hinder the tide that watermen must stay till it rises. When between the bridges the streams are abated, in time no boat will pass; and the river will be destroyed totally for passage, it being already full of shelves.

Putney Bridge emerged over fifty years after these views were voiced. It had been open for seven years when a petition for a bridge at Westminster met with some success in spite of opposition which suggested that self-interest, fear and prejudice were unabated. Counter petitions went to Parliament from the Corporation of London; from the Watermen's Company on account of possible injury to ferries between Vauxhall and the Temple; from the inhabitants of Southwark, claiming that a bridge would injure their trade, ruin the watermen and cause them and their families to fall on the parish; from the lightermen working in the coal craft, detailing the increased difficulties of navigation which a bridge would be likely to cause. Westminster watermen also put in for recompense for injury to their Sunday ferry. Objections printed and circulated at the time included statements that a bridge would raise prices of provisions coming in from the west; would delay and endanger wherries and small craft; would create eddies and sandbanks and would retard the flux of the tide.

The Act 'for building a bridge 'cross the river Thames, from New Palace Yard in the city of Westminster, to the opposite shore, in the county of Surrey' was passed in 1736 and, financed by grants and lotteries, a bridge was built between 1739 and 1750. Compensation for the loss of the ferries was paid to the Watermen's Company and to an organization specifically representing the poor watermen of Westminster, whose finances remained independent of those of the Watermen's Company. A sum was also paid to the Archbishop of Canterbury for the loss of the Horseferry which, incidentally, was the crossing used by King James II when he cast the Great Seal of England into the river as he fled into exile—it being recovered by local peterboat fishermen.

The original proposal had been for a wooden structure with stone piers but when the site came to be chosen in 1738 the Commissioners of the bridge, influenced by recent freeze-ups, came out in favour of a design by Charles Labelye, a naturalized Swiss, for a stone bridge of fifteen arches. A feature of the construction work was a pile-driving engine invented by a watchmaker named Vanloüe. This machine was afterwards described in Cressy's

Encyclopedia of Civil Engineering: 'The engine employed to drive the piles had a ram of 1700 lb., and the height of the striker at a mean was 20 ft. perpendicular; with two horses it gave 45 strokes an hour, and with three horses 70 strokes per hour. When it had worked sufficiently long for the gudgeons or pivots to be rubbed smooth, and the stiffness of the ropes destroyed, three horses going at a common pace gave five strokes in two minutes, the ram being raised from 8 ft. to 10 ft.'

Separate construction contracts were let for various arches and this led to unequal settlement of the bridge piers. After considerable technical delays caused by this, the bridge was finished at a cost of £400,000, which included the approaches. It was opened in November 1750 and for a time at least was the wonder of the age.

Westminster Bridge . . . [according to the annals of the Watermen's Company for 1750] was opened according to notice at midnight, on the seventeenth of November, amidst the sounding of trumpets and kettledrums, accompanied by the discharge of cannon; company came from far and near to admire the beauty of its architecture, and assembled in boats with French horns and other wind instruments, to enjoy the novel effect of the strong echo produced under its semicircular arches.

On Sunday the 18th, the bridge was all day like a fair, from the multitudes going to view the same, it ultimately became impassable, and in the evening the crowd was so great, that a considerable number of persons were compelled to cross the water in boats to get home, the watermen reaping an unexpected harvest.

A curious feature of Labelye's design was the breaking of the bridge balustrades by a series of alcoves in the form of octagonal turrets built over the bridge piers. Structurally these were intended to give additional security to the piers in repelling lateral pressure. Aesthetically they broke the line of the parapet and also served the somewhat dubious practical purpose of sheltering pedestrians. A guide book of the period claimed special acoustic properties for them: 'So just are their proportions, and so complete and uniform their symmetry, that, if a person whispers against the wall on the one side of the way, he may be plainly heard on the opposite side; and parties may converse without being prevented by the inter-

ruption of the street or the noise of carriages.' Unfortunately
these well-intended embellishments became so notorious as cover
for criminals and prostitutes that the bridge commissioners had to
appoint no less than twelve watchmen to keep order at night—a
surprisingly strong body even in those pre-police force days for a
bridge about one thousand feet long.

The doubtful nocturnal reputation of the place did not prevent
William Wordsworth from celebrating its morning view in his
'Upon Westminster Bridge' (1803).

> Earth has not anything to show more fair;
> Dull would he be of soul who could pass by
> A sight so touching in its majesty:
> This City now doth like a garment wear
> The beauty of the morning; silent, bare,
> Ships, towers, domes, theatres, and temples lie,
> Open unto the fields, and to the sky;
> All bright and glittering in the smokeless air.
> Never did sun more beautifully steep
> In his first splendour valley, rock, or hill;
> Ne'er saw I, never felt, a calm so deep!
> The river glideth at his own sweet will:
> Dear God! the very houses seem asleep;
> And all that mighty heart is lying still.

The bridge, which continued under the control of Government
commissioners who were responsible for the toll charges, began to
deteriorate after only half a century of use. Between 1810 and 1838
over £83,000 was spent on maintenance. For the next two decades
constant and costly repairs were made to the failing structure,
nearly all the well-known engineers of the period being called in
for advice. The chief cause of the trouble was the deterioration in
Labelye's foundations and this was accelerated by the scouring
action caused by the removal of the barrage-like structure of Old
London Bridge.

The other important bridge-building enterprise of the eighteenth century was the construction of Blackfriars Bridge. This
did not arouse such passionate controversies as those engendered
by the Putney and Westminster bridges proposals though a bridge
at Blackfriars crossing the well-established ferry routes and so

close to London Bridge might have been expected to have met insurmountable opposition. The Corporation of London sponsored the bridge, the proposal for which was put forward by the city architect in 1750. The Watermen's Company received £12,250 compensation for the abolition of the Sunday ferry, and the claims of a number of ferrymen and market gardeners who made much use of the Blackfriars stairs were met. The Corporation showed considerable enterprise in accepting the design of Robert Mylne (1734–1811), then in his early twenties and just returned from a tour of Europe, having studied architecture in Rome. His design was for a bridge of Portland stone consisting of nine semi-elliptical arches, the centre one 100 feet wide with a rise of nearly 42 feet. Between the arches double Ionic columns supporting small projecting recesses were placed against the face of each pier. The appearance of the young Scotsman's designs caused some literary uproar, both Dr Samuel Johnson and the poet Charles Churchill supporting opposing claims for semicircular arches and iron railings as against stone balustrades for the bridge.

In 1760 while the removal of the houses and the rebuilding of the central arch of old London Bridge were proceeding, the first pile for Blackfriars Bridge was driven into the centre of the river. A day or so later a certain John Blake, in a west country barge—and the west country bargemen were great opponents of bridges—severely damaged the pile in a manœuvre which was described as 'attempting to navigate two barges at one time', for which he was fined £5. The first stone was laid by the Lord Mayor in that year six days after the accession of George III to the throne.

The celebrations included eulogistic references to the Prime Minister and it was unanimously agreed that the finished work should be called William Pitt Bridge. By the time it was completed at a cost of £230,000 and opened in 1768, Pitt's glamour had faded and the bridge was called Blackfriars to commemorate the great Dominican Monastery that had once graced the area at the city end of the bridge. At that period the area had singularly fallen from grace, being notable mainly for its concentration of the four prisons, Ludgate, the Fleet, Newgate and Bridewell, and for the notoriously filthy Fleet ditch which was covered over when the bridge was built.

The funds for the work were raised by a loan on the security of the tolls and of the Bridge House Estate. The loan was to be repaid by tolls levied on the bridge which, until their abolition in the eighteen-seventies, were one halfpenny for every foot passenger, and one penny on Sundays. They were unpopular. For instance in 1778 at a time when a tax on coal in the Port of London was being considered to raise money for bridges and other public works including Newgate Gaol, there was circulated a popular pamphlet entitled 'Reasons for the Immediate Discontinuation of tolls on Blackfriars Bridge'. The writer wound up his discourse with these words: 'It is therefore hoped, that a Toll so disgraceful to one of the principal Entrances into the Metropolis of a great Kingdom, and so burdensome to its Trade and that of the Southern Counties, will not be suffered to continue, but that the Passage over the said Bridge will immediately be made free.'

Two years later the tolls attracted the fury of the Gordon rioters, who singled out Blackfriars Bridge for attack. The tollhouse was burned and all the account books destroyed.

Young Robert Mylne the architect made a great reputation for himself, turning from bridge construction to become Surveyor of St Paul's Cathedral. He built a handsome residence at the northern foot of Blackfriars Bridge, afterwards occupied by the railway station. He could not have felt too happy about his bridge which began to need attention after a very few years and suffered like Westminster Bridge from the tidal changes at London Bridge. Repairs costing £90,000 were carried out in 1803; and in 1860, less than one hundred years after its first opening, the Corporation was inviting designs for a new bridge.

Eighteenth-century bridge-building tended to cater for those who travelled by coach and equipage. Earl Spencer's project for a bridge between Chelsea and Battersea was an example of private enterprise aimed at a new and lucrative development in transportation. The Earl was joined by more than a dozen partners, each of whom took a share in the franchise and in the cost of building the bridge. The arrangements took a long time. The Act of Parliament authorizing the bridge was passed in 1766 but the project itself was not constructed until 1771. Speed of construction made up for the delay. Battersea Bridge was already open for foot passengers by the end of 1771 and the following year it was open for carriage traffic.

The bridge was the freehold property of the proprietors, who each enjoyed a special vote both in the counties of Middlesex and Surrey which the bridge joined. The total cost together with the approach roads was just over £15,600. The shareholders did not do very well, the receipts from the tolls being absorbed by repairs and improvements. In the severe winter of 1795 accumulated ice damaged the bridge and no dividends were paid for the rest of that century. In 1799 oil lamps were installed on one side of the bridge and this pioneering effort in bridge lighting was followed in 1824 when the bridge was illuminated by gas, the pipes being brought over from Chelsea—Battersea remaining without gas for some years afterwards.

The bridge was picturesque enough to be painted by Whistler but from the beginning it was a menace to navigation. Its openings had to be reduced in number and the spans widened by the introduction of iron girders. Apart from expenses such as these the proprietors paid out considerable sums in improving the approach roads in Battersea and on Wandsworth Common. The bridge remained in the hands of the descendants or friends of the original proprietors until the 1870s, when the Metropolitan Board of Works took over.

To the west, Kew Bridge, built somewhat earlier, owed its existence not only to the increasing coach traffic of the century but to the impetus of royal family settlement at Kew. The ferry between Brentford and Kew, the one supposedly used by the Romans, had been for centuries an important strategic and commercial link between the metropolis, the West Country and the Midlands, when Frederick, Prince of Wales, took a lease of a mansion belonging to the Capel family at Kew in 1730. He resided there for some twenty years, enlarging the house and entertaining upon a lavish scale. His presence brought greatly increased traffic to the horse-ferry owned by Robert Tunstall, who carried the suffix 'Gent' and was a Brentford citizen of some consequence. The ferry account book for the period 1734–7 contains almost daily entries such as the following:

His Highness 2 setts 28 horses   9 6
Mr Nutkins a Cart   2 6
The Princes Butchers Cart   1 6
Horse boat cash   19 6
Foot   4 1

In 1757 Robert Tunstall, who had considerable means and influence, applied successfully to Parliament to replace his ferry by a toll bridge. Opposition from barge-owners was strong enough to cause the sanction to be withdrawn. But a new Act followed for the bridge in a more acceptable position. As with Battersea Bridge the construction was amazingly rapid. In less than a year from the laying of the foundation stone the hump-backed bridge, built largely of wood, with a roadway 30 feet wide and having eleven arches, was opened for traffic. The opening day, 4th June 1759, was well chosen, being the birthday of Prince Frederick's son, the future George III, but the royal family had not awaited the official opening. The *London Chronicle* of June 7th stated: 'On Friday last [this would be 1st June] their Royal Highnesses the Prince, and Princess Dowager of Wales with the Royal Family, passed over the new bridge at Kew. His Royal Highness the Prince was pleased to make a present to the proprietor of £200, and ordered 40 guineas to be given to the workmen.' On the opening day some three thousand people crossed the bridge and the one hundred workmen who built it were given a dinner in the evening.

The following year the new bridge was the scene of a significant royal event, when Prince George, riding from Kew Palace with Lord Bute, met a messenger crossing the bridge from London bearing news that George II was dead and that he therefore was King. Walpole described the incident: 'Without surprise or emotion, without dropping a word that indicated what had happened, he said his horse was lame and turned back to Kew. At dismounting, he said to the groom, "I have said that this horse is lame; I forbid you to say the contrary."'

Robert Tunstall, like other bridge proprietors of the eighteenth century, had not taken into sufficient account the high cost of maintenance of a timber structure, and much of his toll money was swallowed up in repairs to the bridge, which nevertheless out-lasted his lifetime. In 1782 his son, also called Robert, obtained

Parliamentary sanction for a stone bridge to the east of the former bridge, to consist of seven arches of which the central arch was to be 65 feet wide. Robert's sister had married the son of John Haverfield, the first superintendent of Kew Gardens, and the Haverfields who eventually inherited the proprietary rights assisted in the financial promotion of the new bridge, funds for which were raised by tontine. Tontine insurances, which were common in the eighteenth century, consisted of annuities shared by the subscribers to a loan, with the benefit of survivorship, the annuities being increased as the subscribers died, until at last the whole went to the last subscriber, or the last two or three, according to the terms on which the money was advanced. The Tontine Insurance document relating to the Kew Bridge is in the British Museum.

A reference to the new bridge was made in *The Diary* of 24th September 1789: 'This beautiful structure was finished on Monday evening, and prepared for His Majesty to pass over, which ceremony was expected on Tuesday, and a great concourse of carriages attended in consequence. Till the Sovereign has been over, the bridge will not be open to carriages, and yesterday, on his return from St. James', he was expected to pass it. Mr. Tunstall and the other proprietors, on Tuesday, gave an elegant dinner to sixty persons at "The Star and Garter", and yesterday the workmen were entertained, The building of this bridge is estimated at £16,000. The King, it is said, proposed to purchase it, and relieve the public of the toll.' A few days later *The Diary* added: 'There will be no more wooden bridges over the Thames, those of Battersea, Putney, &c., which are hastily decaying, will be rebuilt at some future period with stone in every way more beautiful and lasting.'

The King did not in fact buy Kew Bridge, which remained in the control of the Tunstall-Haverfield families until 1819, when it was sold to Thomas Robinson for £20,000, in whose family it remained until it ceased to be a private property in the 1870s. The bridge itself served until the end of the nineteenth century, when it was rather patronizingly described thus in *Engineering* in 1895: 'The bridge possesses no features of engineering or architectural interest; the steep curve given to the roadway is inconvenient for traffic, though characteristic of the period of its design. The piers are probably carried on timber piles, though no information on this point appears to exist. But though not satisfactory as regards its design, Kew Bridge has been so familiar an object to many generations that it has earned its place in popular appreciation as a landmark with many associations.'

The other long-serving stone bridge of the eighteenth century, at Richmond toward the upper extent of the tideway, was built on the site of an ancient ferry. The earliest written records of the ferry's existence were in 1442 and 1480 when the ferrymen were registered. During the sixteenth century the ferry was in the hands of the Sovereign as Lord of the Royal Manor. It was leased for an annual rent of 13s. 4d., usually to a retired retainer from the Royal Household. In 1536 the ferry was rented to John Pate, formerly Keeper of the King's Wardrobe at Greenwich. Elizabeth I granted rights to Thomas Williams late of the 'Boyling House'. Several references in the Privy Purse accounts show that ferrymen prospered particularly when the court travelled by river or resided at Richmond Palace, where Queen Elizabeth died.

In 1662 the ferry was leased by the Crown to Edmund Cooke and Edmund Sawyer, and as the document mentioned their 'Executors, Administrators and Assigns' it appears that the privilege had been converted into a family affair, with rights of inheritance. There were two boats, one for passengers and a much larger vessel, the 'horse boat', for horses, small, light carts and bulky goods. Carriages could not be taken. They had to be driven round to Kingston Bridge.

In 1767 the King granted to William Windham by Letters Patent 'all that passage over the river Thames called Richmond ferry, together with the boats and all and singular the profits to the said ferry belonging, for a term of years, at the yearly rent of three pounds thirteen shillings and four pence.'

By this time Richmond and Twickenham were well established culturally and socially. Alexander Pope had lived for twenty-five years at Twickenham and was buried there. Horace Walpole had set himself up at Strawberry Hill in 1747. Richmond and Twickenham were thriving, well-connected, fashionable and expanding communities: and pressure upon the ferry service grew. Windham enjoyed the benefits of this but also saw advantages to himself in proposals for a bridge. He offered to sell back the unexpired term of his lease of the ferry to the Crown for £6,000 and to apply this money towards building a bridge.

The local inhabitants left the authorities in no doubt about their discontent with the ferry. A publication entitled 'The Case of the Inhabitants of Richmond in respect to a Bridge between Richmond and the opposite Shore' stated that the ferry was 'very inconvenient and at many times impassable by reason of Frosts and Floods and on account of the steepness of the Hill next the Richmond Shore, is never used by loaded Waggons and Carts, which can neither ascend or descend to the Ferry with safety'.

This protest did not blind the residents to the suspicion that Windham was taking advantage of the situation and that the wooden bridge he proposed would be built on the cheap. In February 1772 *Lloyd's Evening Post* printed a letter against Windham's project to throw up his bridge in six months. 'What a cat-stock building this must be, to be executed in so short a time! Methinks I heard Old Thames groan to be so vilely strode. . . . If our view up and down the river must be obstructed for the honour of the counties of Surrey and Middlesex let it be an elegant and free bridge.'

The following year, Windham withdrew his petition to Parliament and plans for a stone bridge were put in hand with a fresh petition to Parliament. Windham now opposed the scheme, claiming that it was being done without his consent and that he required compensation for the loss of his ferry. When the Act was passed for the building of a bridge at the estimated cost of £25,000 Windham was awarded £6,000. The money was raised by tontine shares of £100 each and tolls were to be levied to pay off the shareholders. The promoters took a strict line with potential vandals. A clause was written into the Act stating that anyone causing the slightest damage to the structure of the bridge would be liable for transportation 'to one of His Majesty's Colonies in America for the space of seven years'. The hump-backed bridge was built, 1774–7, of Portland stone with five spans and a carriageway only 16 feet 6 inches wide, the architects being Kenton Couse and James Paine. The last annuitant benefiting from the tolls died in 1859, when the bridge was freed. Painted by Constable and Turner in the last century, improved in width and gradient in this, the old bridge triumphantly survives all contemporaries.

So the eighteenth century closed with half a dozen bridges across the tideway built and operated by private enterprise in addition to the ailing structure of old London Bridge. The Industrial Revolution was consolidating and would make itself felt in a vast expansion of London, especially upon the tideway. The pressures of road transport were building up and steam was on its way in. The turn of the century brought a change of outlook towards the crossing of London's river. Bridges were a challenge which the new building techniques could readily accept.

7

The Nineteenth Century

During the three decades of the nineteenth century before Victoria came to the throne there was much bridge-building activity which reflected the social, industrial and commercial changes in the metropolis.

The first new bridge of the century, that at Vauxhall, was typical of the broader thinking of the period. It was not merely a matter of expediency. Its conception was to attempt to open up in a big way the under-developed south bank of the river. The plans put forward by the Vauxhall Bridge Company therefore included the creation of Vauxhall Bridge Road to make a broad thoroughfare between Hyde Park Corner and the river. Thence by way of the bridge they envisaged an unbroken line of communication through Kennington and the Old Kent Road to Greenwich. The company obtained an Act of Parliament in 1809 sanctioning the construction of the bridge and its approaches. A second Act was obtained three years later after the construction work had started. The first stone on the Middlesex side was laid in 1811 by Lord Dundas representing the Prince Regent, after whom the bridge was to be named. The first stone on the Surrey side was laid two years later by Prince Charles of Brunswick, who was afterwards killed in the Battle of Waterloo. In spite of its grandiose conceptions and these ceremonial occasions, the Bridge Company was embarrassingly short of cash at the outset. The famous Vauxhall

Gardens on the south bank were to continue for half a century as
one of London's entertaining resorts but there had never been any
lack of watermen to ferry people across to enjoy its pleasures, and
the construction of a bridge offered no great financial prospects
on that score. There were few buildings on either side of the
crossing: indeed the only one of consequence was Millbank
prison, which was open for the reception of inmates twelve days
after the public opening of the bridge. The bridge was therefore
a long-term project which did not inspire financial backing in the
early stages of construction.

The company began well by commissioning designs from the
great engineer John Rennie (1761–1821). His plans had been
accepted and work had started under his direction when the
company decided that they could not afford his final estimate
for a stone bridge. Their abandonment of Rennie seemed at the
time to be based solely on financial misgivings, though it subsequently appeared that there were other elements contributing
to the defeat of Rennie's plans. These are not mentioned in the
account of the affair given by his son, Sir John Rennie (1794–
1874).

> At this period [about 1813] Vauxhall Bridge was in course of
> construction, and I was directed by my father to attend to this,
> under Mr. Jones, the resident engineer; but they had scarcely
> finished the Middlesex abutment up to the springing of the first
> arch, and were preparing the caisson for founding the first pier,
> when the company found that they had not sufficient funds to
> carry into effect Mr. Rennie's design, which was very beautiful.
> The bridge was to be made entirely of the fine blue sandstone
> from Dundee, and to consist of seven arches, segments of circles,
> the centre arch being 110 ft. span. . . .

After describing details of his father's proposal he goes on to say:

> This was upon the whole a very elegant, light, and chaste design.
> Finding that the company had not sufficient funds to carry into
> effect the stone design, Mr. Rennie proposed another wholly of
> iron, consisting of 11 arches, with a total waterway of 732 ft.,
> supported upon cast-iron columns filled with masonry, and resting
> upon a platform supported upon piles, and surrounded by sheet-
> ing piles. The centre arch was to be 86 ft. span and 8 ft. rise, and

the others diminishing regularly to each end so as to enable the roadway to be formed into a graceful curve rising 1 in 60. This also was an extremely light, elegant, and economical design. The total cost of this elegant design was estimated at £100,000, and would have been executed first, but at that time even this amount was not forthcoming. The works then stopped, and some time elapsed before the company was resumed, and ultimately constructed the present bridge.

Rennie's original estimate had been for £216,000. The rival estimate which the company accepted had been for only £1,000 less; and it seems probable that Rennie was the victim of some rather shady financial manoeuvring. The final expenditure was about £300,000. To recoup this and to compensate the ferrymen involved, the company was sanctioned to charge a toll of 1*d.* for foot passengers, 2*d.* for beasts and amounts up to 1*s.* 6*d.* for vehicles.

With four architects having a hand in its design the bridge took five years to construct. The result, mainly the work of James Walker, the engineer and contractor, was the first cast-iron bridge over the Thames. It consisted of nine arches all of the same span, springing from stone and brick piers, which were built in caissons and protected by piling, so that the plan originally proposed by Rennie for this part of the work had been closely followed. The gradient of the roadway was described as excessive. Called the Regent Bridge when it opened in 1816, its name was soon changed to Vauxhall Bridge. It was not replaced until the beginning of the twentieth century.

John Rennie was one of the versatile men of his time. He was at once a mathematician and a practical engineer. He was one of those who initiated and pioneered a transportation system which enabled the Industrial Revolution to develop and consolidate. His work was concerned with canals, harbours, drainage schemes, viaducts, tunnels and bridges. He had a hand in three Thames crossings, the reconstructed London Bridge, the first Southwark Bridge and the first Waterloo Bridge. His fame as a bridge-builder rests upon the last of these, which was described by Antonio Canova (1757–1822), the Italian sculptor, as 'the noblest bridge in the world . . . alone worth coming to London to see'.

Like so many of the great pioneers of the period such as Brunel,
Rennie could turn his hand to any aspect of technical calculation
or practical work.

> He never trusted to any assistant [wrote his son], he designed
> everything to the minutest particular with his own hand, specified
> the manner in which it was to be made and specified the price. He
> directed in the same manner every design whether of a bridge, road,
> canal, dock, drainage, or harbour. It was in the first instance
> sketched out by himself, then the mode of construction was speci-
> fied, then estimated, and then the general report explaining the
> whole was written by him. Clerks then merely copied.

Man management was another essential ability which Rennie
shared with other great construction men of the nineteenth
century such as Thomas Brassey and de Lesseps. His son wrote:
'He possessed a wonderful knowledge of mankind and thoroughly
understood how to choose the agents who were to carry out his
work, and they, knowing and appreciating his great talents and
being thoroughly convinced that their services would be well
rewarded, devoted themselves to him and conceived it an honour
to serve under him. He never abandoned them, but did everything in his power to advance their interests.'

Finally, this personal note:

> He was naturally of a quick irritable disposition, so that he felt
> it necessary to keep it under control and schooled himself accord-
> ingly, so that strangers who did not know him were universally
> impressed with his cool, steady and determined behaviour, and
> when he chose nothing could so far provoke him as to exhibit an
> appearance of impatience. . . . He was a general favourite, loved
> and respected by all classes. . . . He was fond of Society and had
> plenty of anecdotes with a good way of telling them. . . .
>
> His personal appearance was very dignified and imposing. He
> was nearly 6 ft 4 ins tall, extremely well proportioned and power-
> fully built, and in his prime could and did walk 50 miles a day
> without fatigue. . . . His head was extremely fine and majestic with
> a broad oval open countenance, large expressive blue eyes, high
> developed forehead, prominent nose slightly curved, with pro-
> portionate mouth and chin, and splendid luxurious auburn hair.
> Sir Thomas Lawrence was going to take his portrait (but died
> before doing so) and said: 'I shall show him as Jupiter for there
> never was a more magnificent head.' Sir Francis Chantrey, who did
> a bust, said that Rennie's head was one of the finest he ever saw.

Rennie's situation over the building of the Strand bridge, as it was first called, was the reverse of that in which he had been placed at Vauxhall. An Act of 1809 incorporated the Strand Bridge Company, who appointed George Dodd to design the bridge. This engineer was the son of Ralph Dodd (1756–1822) who had been much occupied in Thames tunnel construction referred to in Chapter 9. The designs of John Rennie were brought in to supersede those of Dodd, who nevertheless continued to work with Rennie as an assistant. The whole conception was majestic, in keeping with the outlook of the new century. The total length of the works was nearly a mile, of which the bridge itself occupied about a quarter of a mile. The cost with the approaches amounted to nearly one million pounds. The bridge had nine arches elliptical in form, each with a span of 120 feet. The whole of the arches and the exterior face of the bridge were built of Cornish granite from Penryn, with a balustrade of grey Aberdeen granite. Hitherto the gradients of some of the Thames bridges had taxed the horse-drawn vehicles of the day and one of Rennie's especially commendable achievements was that the roadway upon the summit of the arches of the new bridge was level on a line with the Strand and was carried by a gentle declivity over the Surrey bank to the level of the roads in the neighbourhood of the old Surrey Theatre, now the Old Vic.

The first stone was laid in October 1811 with the shadow of Napoleon looming over Europe. When in 1814 the Allied Sovereigns visited Britain the bridge-building works were inspected by the Emperor Alexander I of Russia not once but several times and he declared that the new bridge was the finest work of masonry in the world. The Strand Bridge Company went to Parliament twice more for authority to raise money to be recouped by tolls. On the second occasion, in 1816, the year after the Battle of Waterloo, the Act sanctioned the change of name from Strand to Waterloo Bridge, stating that 'the said bridge when completed will be a work of great stability and magnificence, and such works are adopted to transmit to posterity the remembrance of great and glorious achievements'.

It was duly opened by the Prince Regent on the second anniversary of the Battle of Waterloo, 18th June 1817. He was accompanied by the Duke of Wellington and many of the staff officers who had served in the Battle. After the ceremonies, which were prolonged and magnificent, the Prince Regent expressed his desire to confer a knighthood on John Rennie but the honour was declined. The bridge was subsequently enhanced by the construction of the Embankment, that masterpiece of Victorian town planning. The tolls continued to be collected by the company until the Metropolitan Board of Works bought the bridge in 1877.

Rennie's work on Southwark Bridge, built between 1814 and 1819, to some extent overlapped that of Waterloo Bridge. This cast-iron bridge at Southwark was regarded as the peak achievment in this field of engineering. Some fifty years after its opening Robert Stephenson reported that 'as an example of arch construction, it stands confessedly unrivalled as regards its colossal proportions, its architectural effect, and the general simplicity and massive character of its details'.

Rennie was commissioned to design this bridge by the Southwark Bridge Company, which had been formed to build a bridge on a site which was the narrowest part of the river between London and Blackfriars bridges. The promoters had met with great opposition from the City Corporation and from the Thames Conservators, at that time the governing body of the waterway. History was to prove that the objections raised to the siting of the bridge in its relation to the street patterns of London and Southwark were justified. The objection that was also raised that the work might constrict the waterway and become a hazard to navigation was to a large extent met by Rennie's design for a bridge consisting of three arches. The centre of these was 240 feet wide, the two side arches were 210 feet.

During the later decades of the eighteenth century cast-iron bridge-building had been successfully developed and there were precedents for Rennie, whose work nevertheless was the most ambitious of its kind. There was the famous Coalbrookdale bridge across the Severn built during 1777-9. In 1790 Thomas Payne had invented a cast-iron bridge which was built at Rotherham and erected for exhibition in London. Part of this was used in 1795 for the famous Sunderland bridge erected by Roland Burden.

The six thousand tons of iron required at Southwark were cast at Rotherham. Rennie took immense pains to find the right masonry and sent one of his sons to seek suitable materials. Aberdeen could not supply the large blocks required but at Peterhead the younger Rennie discovered a single block of twenty-five tons which he managed to transport to the harbour. With great difficulty he induced the captain of a cargo steamer to bring it to London. Having made this trial run the Rennies continued to obtain supplies of granite from Peterhead. The outer facing of piers and abutments of hard siliceous stone was obtained from quarries near Edinburgh and Dundee. The ceremonial opening of the bridge was unique and dramatic. On the evening of 24th March 1819 it was illuminated with lamps and declared open to the public 'as the clock of St. Paul's tolled midnight'.

It was never a satisfactory bridge. During half a century it earned tolls for the company which built it but failed to relieve the burden of traffic on London and Blackfriars bridges. It suffered from bad approaches on the south bank and lack of communication with the main arteries of the city on the north bank. The gradients were steep, one in twenty-eight on the southern side and one in nineteen on the northern. The roadway was only just over 28 feet wide. Not long after its construction it was calculated to be carrying only one fortieth of the traffic using London Bridge.

We have already referred to the start of the rebuilding of London Bridge, which was the elder Rennie's posthumous work. It took nearly seven and a half years, and the cost, including the approaches, was nearly one and a half million pounds—and forty lives. These high casualties may well have been due to the fact that the building of the new bridge had to be carried out alongside the old one. Sir John Rennie, the son who completed the work and was knighted for it, wrote:

It consists of five semi-elliptical arches; two are of 130 feet, two of 140 feet, and the centre, of 152 feet 6 inches span and 37 feet 6 inches rise, is perhaps the largest elliptical arch ever attempted. The roadway is 52 feet wide. This bridge deserves remark on account of the difficult situation in which it was built, being immediately above the old bridge, in depth of from 25 to 30 feet at low water, on a soft alluvial bottom, covered with large loose

stones carried away by the force of the current from the foundation of the old bridge, the whole of which had to be removed by
dredging before the cofferdams for the piers and abutments could
be commenced, otherwise it would have been extremely difficult,
if not impracticable, to have made them water-tight. The difficulty was further increased by the old bridge being left standing
to accommodate the traffic whilst the new bridge was building;
and the restricted waterway of the old bridge occasioned such an
increased velocity of the current as materially to retard the
operations of the new bridge, and at times the tide threatened to
carry away all before it. The great magnitude and extreme flatness
of the arches demanded unusual care in the selection of the
materials, which were of the finest blue and white granite from
Scotland and Devonshire. The piers and abutments stand upon
platforms of timber resting upon piles about 20 feet long. The
masonry is from 8 feet to 10 feet below the bed of the river.

For the opening ceremony King William IV commanded that
there should be a procession by water 'with the double view of
benefiting the men employed on the river and of enabling the
greatest number of his subjects to witness the spectacle', according
to a contemporary record. A magnificent pavilion was erected,
extending over the whole width of the bridge, and the throne was
placed in the royal tent at the city end. The actual opening was
performed by the King and Queen walking over the bridge where
on the Surrey side they witnessed the ascent of a Mr Green 'in
his celebrated balloon' (which descended that evening at Charl-
wood in Surrey). Then there was the dinner at which the King
was presented with a gold cup. The sailor king managed an
eloquent toast: 'I cannot but refer on this occasion to the great
work which has been accomplished by the citizens of London. The
City of London has been renowned for its magnificent improvements, and we are commemorating a most extraordinary instance
of their skill and talent. I shall propose the source from whence
this vast improvement sprang: "The trade and commerce of the
City of London".'

At least one person present had a thought for the work of Peter
de Colechurch. She was Lucy Aikin, a journalist, who wrote:

I was present, a few days ago, at the splendid spectacle of the
opening of new London Bridge. It was covered half-way over with

a grand canopy, formed of the flags of all nations, near which His Majesty dined with about two thousand of his loyal subjects. The river was thronged with gilded barges and boats, covered with streamers, and crowded with gaily dressed people; the shores were alive with the multitude. In the midst of the gay show I looked down the stream upon the old, deserted, half-demolished bridge, the silent remembrancer of seven centuries.

The contractors for the building of the bridge and the removal of the old bridge were Messrs Jolliffe and Banks, who had also been the builders of Southwark and Waterloo bridges. They received £10,000 and the old material for the demolition of old London Bridge, and it was their men who uncovered the remains of Peter de Colechurch, and perhaps unceremoniously disposed of them. Little attempt was made to conserve any of the medieval stonework except for small items kept as curiosities scattered about the country.

It was a curious irony that the senior partner of the contractors was, like Peter de Colechurch, a clerk in Holy Orders. The Reverend William Jolliffe had given up the pulpit to become a contractor and make a fortune. He was living at Merstham, Surrey, when he first made the acquaintance of Banks, who was working as a navvy on the Surrey Iron Railway extension through Merstham. Somehow the clergyman and the navvy went into partnership, which became one of the most successful contracting businesses of the time. It earned Banks a knighthood. In the churchyard at Chipstead his tomb is inscribed, 'Sir Edward Banks, the builder of the three noblest bridges in the world—London, Southwark and Waterloo.'

Some idea of the prosperity enjoyed by parson-builder Jolliffe is reflected in the unique specially printed, leather-bound and silver-clasped volume to commemorate the building of London Bridge which he commissioned and paid for. The book is in the possession of his family—with the receipt still tucked inside it. It cost him £347—no mean sum in 1836.

Outside the Metropolitan area there was one other nineteenth-century bridge built before Queen Victoria came to the throne, that at Hammersmith. Opened in 1827, it was the first suspension bridge erected in the south of England. It was a light and inexpensive structure, with a 20-foot-wide roadway occupying the site of the present bridge. One of the features incorporated in the structure was the mid-channel steamboat pier enabling the new steamers to operate their services where there was sufficient water at all states of the tide. This was one of the earliest specifically structural acknowledgments of the coming of steam to the river.

A private company built the bridge and for half a century it served its purpose well and provided a good return for the shareholders. Only two years after it opened the Oxford and Cambridge Boat Race started on the tideway as an annual event, and Hammersmith Bridge from the beginning offered a first-rate grandstand view. This provided a profitable bonus in tolls for the shareholders but was thought to be bad for the bridge. By the seventies, when the structure was beginning to cause anxiety, it was estimated that it carried between eleven and twelve thousand spectators on Boat Race Day, and this was officially cited as one of the causes of its deficiencies. Its replacement in the eighties will be described in Chapter 11 (p. 127).

8

The Railways Arrive

The *Observer* in June 1837, the year Queen Victoria came to the throne, recorded that: 'The public are now able to avail themselves of the River Thames as a highway, and secure a healthful, safe, quick, and economical conveyance between Westminster Bridge, Hungerford Market, and London Bridge, by means of commodious steamboats.'

By this time steam locomotion had already been established on the river for two decades. In 1815 George Dodd had bought and fitted out a steam vessel in Glasgow, which he brought to London for pleasure trips on the tideway. This pioneering enterprise started a boom in which steamboat companies proliferated, with cut-throat competition and little regard for safety. The steamer exploitation of the Thames tideway was a nineteenth-century phenomenon which soon dwindled as competition from railways and better road services increased. The steamboat passenger boom was in fact the swansong of the Thames tideway as what had been called the silent highway of the metropolis.

With the bridges subject to toll and road development still primitive, the public took eagerly to the new steamboat services both as a means of crossing the river and travelling up and down stream.

The steamboat companies on the Thames [writes H. P. Clunn], owing to the absence of any control, did exactly as they liked in those days, although omnibus proprietors and owners of cabs were numbered and licensed. Thus what was punishable in the Strand was permitted on the river, though in practice the river was a hundred times more dangerous. In the absence of any proper landing-places the companies erected long lines of rickety piers made of dirty barges planked over, at any spot that suited their convenience. Sometimes two rival companies placed their piers side by side, so that the public were constantly deluded into taking wrong tickets for the boat which never came along. All along the river the piers were an eyesore, a public nuisance, and an obstruction.

Thus the age of steam gave the river, somewhat briefly, new significance as a much-used and misused thoroughfare: yet the tideway became more and more an impediment to communication between north and south not only to social life and trade but in the daily movements of a vastly increasing working population. During the first twenty years of Victoria's reign the only toll-free crossings for those who went to work on foot were over London, Blackfriars and Westminster bridges.

To the present generation [wrote G. A. Sekon in 1938], with its quick means of locomotion and absence of bridge-tolls, it may seem surprising that the payment of a halfpenny to cross a bridge was a daily deciding factor with tens of thousands of pedestrians as to the route they adopted in reaching their destinations. Money was of greater value three-quarters of a century ago than now; wages were less and everything was performed in more leisurely fashion. There is another aspect of the matter. The value of the time spent and the shoe-leather disintegrated on the less direct route must in the case of many pedestrians have exceeded the amount of toll.

Some of the new pedestrian pressure was met when a company was formed to erect a footbridge between Hungerford Market, close to Charing Cross, and what was described as the 'worst part' of Lambeth. The Hungerford suspension bridge was designed by Isambard Kingdom Brunel. The centre span was 676 feet and the total length of the bridge was 1,352 feet. An important element in the young Brunel's design was the use of the two piers as landing-stages for the steamboats, passengers making their way by stairs to the footbridge level. Until the building of the Embankment later in that century it was impossible for steamboats at all

states of the tide to operate inshore at such points as Charing
Cross.

Hungerford Bridge, which was opened in 1845, was the first
new bridge across the tideway in the Victorian era. It operated
as a toll-bridge for nearly two decades and was popular, more
than ten thousand people a day using it. In the 1860s it was
purchased by the South-Eastern Railway and incorporated in the

Steamboats at London Bridge in 1859; paper-seller in the foreground.

railway bridge, Brunel's original piers being retained to this day
on the downstream side of the bridge.

When Hungerford suspension bridge opened Queen Victoria
had already taken her first ride in a railway train—with Brunel
sharing the footplate with Daniel Gooch—and had expressed
herself 'quite charmed with it'. The Queen was using the Great
Western railway between Slough and London, where there was
already a passenger terminus convenient to the West End at
Paddington. The Thames was yet unbridged by the new railroads. Passengers approaching the metropolis from the south
terminated their journeys at Nine Elms, then an unpopulated spot

on the banks of the Thames about a mile and a half south-west of Westminster Bridge. The railway erected a pier at Nine Elms so that steamers could link passengers with the north bank and the centre of the city. So little advantage was taken of this in the early days that the railway had to advertise for steamboat owners to tender for a service to coincide with up and down trains for Southampton.

The extension of that line to Portsmouth in 1839, the change of its title to the London and South Western railway and the building of a new terminus at Waterloo were the signal for the first railway crossings of the river.

Aesthetically the bridges were calamitous. The railways bridged the Thames more or less where it suited them and very few protests were made at their unseemliness or ineptitude. Only occasionally a critical voice was raised. 'The entire invention of the designer,' wrote Ruskin of Blackfriars railway bridge 'seems to have exhausted itself in exaggerating to an enormous size a weak form of iron nut, and in conveying the information upon it, in large letters, that it belongs to the London, Chatham & Dover Railway Company.'

The first railway crossing was the bridge at Richmond, opened in 1848, to serve what *Punch*, in a dazzling moment of wit, described as 'the London and Datchet *Snailway*'. Neither this bridge nor the one that followed it was constructed specifically to give the railroads access to the metropolis. Their purpose was rather to enable the growing network to spread. The second bridge built in 1849 at Barnes was to cater for a loop line from Richmond to Hounslow. Still considered, even as a matter of local pride, to be the ugliest crossing of the tideway, the bridge was in its original form designed by Joseph Locke and built by Thomas Brassey's army of navvies.

Its completion was held up for a month owing to the fact that a cottage in Back Lane, Barnes, now called Malthouse Passage, doomed for demolition, was occupied by an expectant mother who could not be moved. The child who was safely delivered after delaying the engineering work was Abraham Badham, who benefited by the railway to the extent of opening the first fish-monger's shop in Barnes, where the family continued to flourish in this century. The first passenger train steamed across what was then described as the 'light and elegant iron bridge' on Wednesday 22nd August 1849, four years after the first Oxford and Cambridge Boat Race, with which the bridge has since been inseparably associated. The bridge was not beautified by the additions which were made in the nineties.

The first metropolitan crossing was that of the Victoria Station and Pimlico Railway Company, which obtained authority to build a bridge at Pimlico in 1857. The engineer of the bridge was Sir John Fowler, and it was remarkable for the rapidity of its construction, the first stone being laid on 1st June 1859 and the first train passing over it on 9th June 1860. At the time it was the widest railway bridge in the world, being 132 feet wide and 900 feet long—and it was widened again a century later by British Railways. It served both the London, Brighton and South Coast Railway and the London, Chatham and Dover Railway, both companies being tenants at a fixed rental.

There followed at the beginning of the sixties an aggressive surge of railway building from the south. Victoria having replaced Battersea as the new London terminus of the London, Brighton and South Coast Railway, the London, Chatham and Dover Railway Company, then at its zenith, was eager to find a metropolitan terminus of its own, and obtained sanction by a Bill passed in 1860 for a very extensive scheme involving the building of a bridge at Blackfriars, contingent upon the rebuilding of Mylne's road bridge, which was already unsatisfactory. The extent of the operation was thus described in *Engineering*:

> . . . the company was empowered to construct 14 miles of railway, much of which ran through crowded and valuable property on the southern side of the river, to say nothing of those [then] remote suburbs of Loughborough-road, Brixton, and the rest, and which owe their present dimensions mainly to the construction of the railways sanctioned under this Act. The new extension commenced near Beckenham, and followed the well-known route to Dulwich, where it was divided, one branch running towards Victoria, the other passing through Camberwell, Walworth, and Newington, finally arriving at the Thames a short distance below Blackfriars road bridge. The site was, in a sense, unfortunate for the company. That the old Blackfriars Bridge of Mylne was to be removed, and

replaced by a sounder and more worthy structure, had been decided on in principle, but not in detail, and the permission to place a railway bridge across the river at the site selected was made contingent on the condition that its spans should correspond with those of the new road bridge. This condition was a very necessary one in the interests of navigation, which might have been endangered by the close proximity of the two structures. The design for the new road bridge was not settled till two years later, and the commencement of the railway bridge works was consequently postponed till 1862.

The first train crossed Blackfriars Bridge in October 1864 from the old Blackfriars Station, which was on the south bank. A station at Ludgate Hill was opened the following year (it was closed in 1929, bombed in 1941) and the Railway connected with the Great Northern by way of the famous bridge across Ludgate Hill, which has so often been praised or reviled for enhancing or ruining the view of St Paul's.

The next railway crossing of the Thames, which immediately followed that at Blackfriars, was one of the most expensive essays in railway-building in history. Not to be outdone by the achievement of the London, Chatham and Dover Railway in crossing into the city, the South Eastern Railway Company, whose system terminated at London Bridge, decided on two railheads across the river at Charing Cross and at Cannon Street. Sir John Hawkshaw was the designer of both bridges. That at Charing Cross, as we have mentioned already (see p. 83) involved the purchase of Brunel's suspension bridge, at a cost of £40,000 with an additional £85,000 for the toll franchise. During the construction of the railway bridge the toll footway across the river was maintained at all times. Of Brunel's work some of the suspension apparatus was sold for £5,000 for incorporation later in the Clifton Suspension Bridge, while the bases of the two towers of the suspension bridge were used as piers in the new bridge. It consisted of nine spans, providing at first four rail tracks with a footbridge on each side, later increased to six rail tracks with a single footbridge remaining on the downstream side.

The building of the station and the bridge involved the purchase and demolition of Hungerford Market, a large two-storey building which had been opened early in the eighteen-thirties for the sale of

1. *London's River in the seventies*

2. ABOVE: *Old London Bridge (1209–1832) in its heyday, depicted by Visscher about 1632, complete with severed heads at the Southwark approach*

3. TOP RIGHT: *Frost fair, 1683, with watermen manhandling their craft*

4. BOTTOM RIGHT: *Frost fair, 1814, recorded by Cruikshank, with badge-wearing waterman promoting skittles*

5. ABOVE: *The horse-ferry at Lambeth (c. 1706–10). Artist unknown*

6. BELOW: *Rowlandson's caption (1812) ran: 'Entering upon any of the bridges of London, or any of the passages leading to the Thames, being assailed by a groupe of watermen holding up their hands and bawling out: Oars Sculls. Sculls. Oars Oars.'*

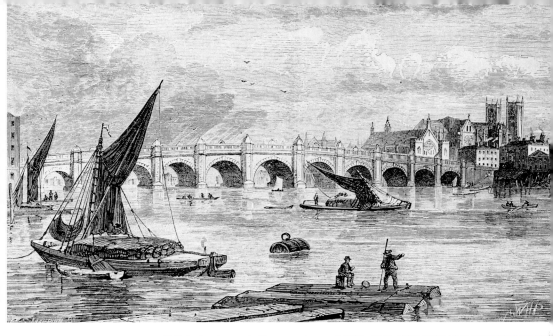

7. ABOVE : *Old Westminster Bridge in 1754*

8. BELOW : *Old Battersea Bridge depicted by H. and W. Greaves in 1860*

9. ABOVE: *The Prince Regent and the Duke of Wellington at the opening of Waterloo Bridge, 1817*

10. BELOW: *Vauxhall Bridge in 1821*

11. ABOVE: *Hammersmith Bridge on Boat Race Day, by Walter Greaves*

12. BELOW: *Old Putney Bridge in 1880*

13. ABOVE: *Rennie's London Bridge, now shipped to America, being built alongside the old bridge, 1828*

15. TOP RIGHT: *Building the Victoria railway bridge in the eighteen-sixties*

16. CENTRE: *Charing Cross railway bridge with steamer pier before construction of the embankment*

17. BOTTOM RIGHT: *Nineteenth-century divers working on Blackfriars Bridge construction*

14. BELOW: *Horse-drawn traffic on London Bridge*

18. TOP LEFT: *Barnes railway bridge in 1849*

19. CENTRE LEFT: *Richmond railway bridge in 1848*

20. BOTTOM LEFT: *Strand-on-the-Green railway bridge, 1867*

21. ABOVE: *The drama of the diving bell above the Thames Tunnel after the flooding of May 1827*

22. BELOW CENTRE: *A German artist's impression of Brunel's tunnelling work*

23. BELOW FOOT: *Brunel's Tunnel opened to foot passengers as one of the sights of London*

24. LEFT ABOVE: *Construction of the Tower Subway. Advancing the shield*

25. LEFT BELOW: *The Tower Subway finished*

26. BELOW: *Artist's (optimistic) impression of carriage to be used in Tower Subway*

27. TOP RIGHT: *Construction work on the Tower Bridge*

28. BOTTOM RIGHT: *Section of the Thames Embankment, 1867*
Showing (1) *The subway*
        (2) *The low-level sewer*
        (3) *The Metropolitan District Railway*
        (4) *The Pneumatic Railway*

29. ABOVE: *The flags out for the opening of Woolwich Free Ferry, 1889*

30. BELOW: *The first horse-drawn vehicles on Woolwich Free Ferry*

31. ABOVE: *Traffic controller at Dartford Tunnel*

32. BELOW: *Traffic electronically controlled in Dartford Tunnel*

33, 34. ABOVE AND BELOW: *London Bridge built up again, 1970–2*

produce. Ironically the *Gentleman's Magazine* at the time had held out hopes that steam would bring trade rather than doom to the market.

> It may now, however, be anticipated with confidence that this propinquity to water-carriage will make the situation particularly convenient for the sale of fish, and the removal of London Bridge will allow the vessels to come up, which was before impracticable. Thus an effectual remedy will be provided against the monopoly of that article which has been too long tolerated at Billingsgate.

So the market was swept away and the bridge works begun in 1860 were completed in 1863 at a total cost of £180,000. But the extravagance which gave London its most ungainly bridge did not rest upon the cost of the structure alone. More expensive than the acquisition of the market on the north bank was the obstacle of St Thomas's Hospital, then a neighbour of Guy's, which stood between London Bridge terminus and the desired objectives. The Hospital Governors stood out for purchase of their entire establishment. After arbitration the sum fixed was £296,000—and the Hospital was rebuilt facing the Houses of Parliament, to be rebuilt again in the latter part of the present century. On its way to Charing Cross the new line made a connection with the London and South Western Railway at Waterloo Junction. Thence the first trains were crossing the river into Charing Cross in 1864.

The following year they were running over Hawkshaw's other bridge into Cannon Street, upon the site of one of the more romantic royal incidents. For it was at the stairs just about here where the rectangular Victorian Gothic towers of Cannon Street station loom over the tideway, that Queen Elizabeth I landed, having been rowed across incognito with only two of her ladies, to meet the Earl of Leicester.

This was a wider bridge, with nine tracks, over a narrower part of the river. At first it incorporated a public footway subject to toll, but this was closed by the railway company in 1877 when the Metropolitan Board of Works obtained toll-extinguishing legislation.

The building of Cannon Street Bridge was an instance where the proximity of noble buildings and an historical setting weighed with the railway engineer. Apart from the 4,200 tons of wrought iron needed for the superstructure, Hawkshaw provided well over a thousand tons of decorative cast iron. The classical ornamentation was lavish. The columns of his piers were fluted and the outer ones carried Doric capitals. Altogether the new bridge was felt at the time to be dressed in a manner worthy of the company of St Paul's Cathedral—and it cost £193,000. Like Charing Cross it was widened in after years.

Meanwhile the engineers of the Great Western and the London and North-Western Railways worked together to create the West London Extension Railway, which was to connect their lines with Victoria Station. This entailed the building of a railway bridge at Battersea, crossing the river on the skew and consisting of five segmented arches. The bridge was designed by the chief engineers of the two railways concerned and opened for traffic in 1863. It carried the broad gauge of the Great Western Railway until that was abolished. Though it was built to relate to Victoria Station the main interest in the line over the bridge is that it provides one of the few direct railway contacts between the north and south of England. This was appreciated by the Germans in World War II, who singled out the bridge as a special target.

Finally, the expansionist railway activities of the 1860s bridged the river, to the lasting annoyance of Zoffany's successors living at Strand-on-the-Green, between Gunnersbury and Kew Gardens stations. Kew Railway Bridge, designed by W. R. Galbraith was, like Battersea, built by Brassey and Ogilvy. Consisting of five spans, it was promoted by the South Western Railway Company as part of their branch between Kensington and Richmond.

There was a lull in railway bridge-building in London for nearly two decades, the pattern of railways having been consolidated and the London termini established. The further building in the eighties was not particularly significant. In 1884 a second bridge was built alongside the existing railway bridge at Blackfriars. It was called St Paul's Bridge of the London, Chatham and Dover Railway Company, and was designed by J. Wolfe Barry and by H. M. Brunel, son of Isambard Kingdom Brunel, afterwards associated together over the Tower Bridge. They provided an elegant iron bridge, the middle span of which corresponds with the older railway bridge. It was opened for traffic in 1886.

Three years later the last of the Victorian railway bridges was laid between Fulham and Putney. This trellis-girder iron bridge was built for the London and South Western Railway and designed by their chief engineer William Jacomb. Fulham Railway Bridge opened in 1889 and was later used by the District Railway for their traffic between Earl's Court and Wimbledon, and it is now part of the London Transport underground system. A footbridge connects with it.

9

Tunnels Attempted

From the railway and road bridge-building in the earlier part of the nineteenth century it might seem that London was developing along the river only to the west of the Tower. This was far from being the case. Growth to the east was as dynamic but it was of a different character, a vast industrial complex of docks, warehouses, manufacturers and trade with a dense spread of mainly working-class population. The tideway east of London Bridge became one of the greatest ports in the world. The river, increasingly polluted, subdued to industrial needs, also became more and more of an obstacle to the flow of road traffic.

> The water-borne commerce of London was a bar to bridges down-river east of London's Bridge [wrote G. A. Sekon]. Over-water facilities for pedestrians were not available. The steamboats crossing from side to side partly filled the gap, and watermen at the numerous stairs on both sides of the river were available to act as ferrymen. On the north bank of the river, east of the Tower to Limehouse Dock, a distance of 2 miles, there were twenty-three stairs, as well as a horseferry, available to the public. Between the Tower and London Bridge were wharves, the Custom House, embankments, Billingsgate, &c. On the south side for the same distance below London Bridge were twenty-seven stairs and also the horseferry.

An alternative method of crossing, without dependence upon

weather and tide, was by tunnelling: and this had been in men's minds even in the previous century.

The notion of a Thames tunnel was first broached at the end of the eighteenth century by Ralph Dodd (1756–1822), a civil engineer and publicist. He was known for canal-building projects. He had written a book entitled *Account of the principal Canals in the known World*. He was an impassioned propagandist against drinking water taken from the Thames. Though some of his views and projects were somewhat outlandish, Ralph Dodd was no freak. Britain was beginning to feel the need of greater mobility to meet the geographical explosion of the Industrial Revolution. So Ralph Dodd got a good hearing when he addressed a paper to the gentry of Kent and Essex with this preamble: 'In the course of my professional travelling, I have observed the want of a grand, uninterrupted line of communication in the south-east part of the Kingdom, which would easily be obtained if the River Thames could be conveniently passed.'

He and others pointed out that goods arriving at the new docks on the north bank destined for the mills, manufacturers and warehouses in the south had to make the slow and tortuous journey through narrow streets to the Tower, over old London Bridge, paying a toll, and onward through Southwark and Rotherhithe to their destination. It was sometimes claimed that to carry a cargo of skins across the Thames from Wapping cost more than bearing them across the Atlantic from Hudson Bay. At the time when Ralph Dodd took up this question there were also strong defence considerations. A military link between Kent and Essex might be of immense value in the deployment of troops in the event of a French invasion. So what better point for the construction of a tunnel than between Tilbury Fort, important as an ordnance depot on the Essex shore, and Gravesend, vital as a traditional source of communication with the Channel ports. Dodd's project for a tunnel was stated by *The Times* in July 1798 to 'save a circuitous route of 50 miles by land; (distance from Gravesend to Tilbury, crossing London Bridge)'. The report went on to explain that the tunnel would 'be constructed wholly with keystones; therefore the greater the pressure the stronger will be the work. The diameter to be 16 feet in the clear. . . . The expense of this stupendous undertaking is estimated at so low a sum as £15,995 for 900 yards of tunnelling, relaying the bottom, lamps, lamp-irons, steam-engine, pipes and other necessary machinery. . . .' Ralph Dodd's own breakdown of his figure is not without interest:

900 yards running measure of tunnelling, including excavating and vaulting, with key-stones, etc. at £12 per yard	£10,800
To relaying the bottom with new-made ground, 900 running yards at £1 per yard	£900
To fixing lamps and lamp irons through the tunnel, toll collectors' rooms, gates, etc. at each end	£400
To making good entrance roads at each end of tunnel	£160
To a steam engine, pipes, etc. if found necessary to draw off drainage water	£1,780
To necessary machinary during execution	£500
To 10 per cent upon the whole, for contingencies	£1,455
	£15,995

From the sale of chalk and flints from the excavations, Dodd was confident he could reduce the total figure by some £3,000. . . .

The Board of Ordnance regarded the 'continuous land travel' to be afforded by the tunnel to be valuable for the passage of troops and military stores of all kinds, and by the summer of 1798 Dodd had obtained the support of Colonel Twiss and Captain Holloway of the Royal Engineers, who, with one eye no doubt on Napoleon rampaging in Europe, recommended an early start of the work. Only Charles Clarke of the Gravesend Ordnance office had reservations. When Dodd suggested that the estimated cost might be reduced to £10,000 by reducing the tunnel to a smaller bore taking only one single line of traffic, Clarke's objection was wryly realistic: 'When a carriage enters, a bell is to be rung by Mr. Collector, this is a sign to his colleague at the other extremity who now knows a vehicle has begun its progress (through the tunnel) and he lays a prohibition on the progress of every other till the first emerges. Little urgent must be the business and patient must be the Driver should a second vehicle enter in the same way.'

Dodd ran a number of public meetings to promote the tunnel. After the first, held at Gravesend Town Hall under the chairmanship of the local landowner, the Earl of Darnley, a committee was formed which included three Members of Parliament, Colonel Twiss and a Royal Navy officer and a Gravesend man, John Mills Evans, as secretary. None of them seems to have doubted the practicability of the venture in spite of the fact that at that time no tunnel had ever been made through a river's soft bed except for the almost legendary activity of Queen Semiramis in Babylon, which was widely quoted in a translation which had just been made from Diodorus the Sicilian.

There were, however, objections; that of the *Gentleman's Magazine* had a literary flavour: 'We are invited down a steep ravine to leave the warm precincts of the cheerful day to enter regions of utter darkness and cold obstruction and to grope by lamplight through a deep, close, suffocating, wet gully of frightful extent, with a tremendous body of water over our heads, menacing us, like the Sword of Dionysus, all the way.'

Charles Clarke was again realistic:

It certainly must follow of course, that by expending a large sum of money, a very large and long hole may be bored under ground. But in this case, the expenses of completing this work do by no means end, the moment its bricks and stones are laid. Toll-houses must be erected; toll-keepers employed; lamps must be constantly burning at a very considerable expence;—when to the interest of the capital expended these further additional yearly charges are annexed; there seems to be no reasonable expectation of its turning out to be a work that will pay for itself. The interests of the shores of Kent and Essex can never be deeply engaged in a trading point of view with each other, by this or any other new channel of communication. Their market is the Metropolis, and the surface of the Thames the cheapest road to it. Essex possesses no one commodity which Kent wants. The only trade now existing between the two Counties is, for the chalk which Kent sends to Essex; and as long as a barge can swim, it will always be cheaper to convey bulky commodities from shore to shore, on the surface of the water, than by land under it. It has been said aloud and much relied on, that where a new communication is made from one part of a County to another, that it is a fresh channel in which a new trade will run. When this happens, it must arise from one part of the country being in possession of a saleable article wanted by the other; and for the passing of which this new channel is opened. Now this tunnel except for the passage of troops, is only preparing two roads, one under that river in addition to one where a passage over it is established, and confining it purely to a pecuniary remuneration of its own expences, it must remain a doubt whether the public will prefer the passage of the tunnel to that of the boats; and in proportion as the public is divided in opinion and preference, in such proportion must the future produce of the tunnel be increased or injured.

Undeterred by this, the supporters of the scheme held a meeting in November 1798 at the Crown and Anchor Tavern in the Strand, at which The Thames Archway Company was launched, books being opened to the value of £30,000 in shares of £100. It was followed by another meeting in February 1799, at which it was reported that the whole of the £30,000 had been subscribed. It was also agreed at this meeting that a Samuel Wyatt should be engaged to join Dodd as consultant, a move which was to reflect on the authority of Dodd and to lead to bad working relations. In a subsequent comment in *Notes and Queries* it was suggested that Wyatt would never have been employed if the meetings had taken place at Gravesend where Dodd was master of the situation, and that 'when they drifted into such holes and corners as the Crown and Anchor in the Strand, poor honest, simple-minded Dodd . . . was left in the cold and other and more sinister engineers and schemists were called in to advise'.

In July 1799 George III gave his consent to 'An Act for making and maintaining a Tunnel or Road under the River Thames from or near to the town of Gravesend in the County of Kent to or near to Tilbury Fort in the County of Essex'. The Act did not precisely stipulate the whereabouts of the proposed tunnel but the site chosen was at the western end of Gravesend close to a chalk pit known as The Old Main. There a shaft was sunk under the direction of Colonel Twiss, Samuel Wyatt and a skilled miner named Ludlam. Dodd was absent, whether from pique or because he was not invited is not known. Wyatt and Ludlam continued to carry out the practical work.

After many borings they decided to sink a 10-foot diameter well but when this reached a depth of 42 feet it became so flooded that a steam pump had to be employed to clear it. Already in 1800 Colonel Twiss had warned the company that he could see little possibility of the work being finished in the anticipated time, by the close of 1802. In fact by June 1802 the flooding had become so bad that John Rennie was called in to survey the works and to make a general report. He found that the shaft had reached a point 9 feet below the deepest section of the river bed. For some reason the engine had been stopped and 60 feet of water had percolated into the shaft. When the engine was started the water was cleared in two hours but within one hour of the pump being stopped the water came back. Rennie recommended that the shaft be driven 70 feet lower, and until this was done he declined to hazard an opinion either on practicability or the final cost of the operation. For a month or so his advice was followed but in October 1802 fire destroyed the engine-house and the work was again halted. It began again in December, when the shaft reached a depth of 85 feet. At that point operations may be said to have stumbled to a close but not before Charles Clarke had said his last word: 'the foundations of the desired passage beneath the Thames are neither laid in profoundness of thought nor the depth of professional talent.'

Dodd was not criticized in the reports of Rennie, possibly because the two men were already associated in the plans of what was ultimately Waterloo Bridge. The last report made by the directors of the company contained the following financial statement

Payments	£3,584 0s 0d
Expenses	£9,844 4s 1d
Unsatisfied claims	£5,398 6s 3d

To this there was a sad postscript scribbled on a slip of paper after the final meeting: 'Total cost of the Well, £15,242 10s 4d.'

It was a period of speculation in thought, in money and in skill. The tideway east of London Bridge developed faster than ever after the turn of the century. 'The Victualling Office and Naval Arsenals of Deptford and Woolwich', wrote Henry Law a few years later with some understatement, 'together with the extensive docks, the numerous manufactories, ship builders, coast wharfingers, and other traders on both banks, rendered a land communication eastwards of London Bridge not only highly desirable, but almost necessary.'

There were certainly inducements: and in 1802, before work on Dodd's shaft had come to an end, Robert Vazie, a Cornish mining engineer nicknamed 'the Mole', was circulating a proposal for a tunnel between Rotherhithe and Limehouse. The suggested site was only four miles below London Bridge, wonderfully well placed for serving the new docks in process of being built. Though it might miss the military traffic from Tilbury Fort and all the agricultural and coach traffic between Essex and Kent, the new site clearly had good industrial possibilities. So when Vazie made borings on both sides of the river and reported gleefully 'that the work would not be so expensive as had been expected', financial support was readily forthcoming. A private Act of Parliament was obtained in July 1805 'for making and maintaining an archway or archways under the River Thames from the Parish of Saint Mary Rotherhithe, in the County of Surrey, to the opposite Side of the said River in the County of Middlesex'.

The proposed tunnel was to be 'passable for Horses, and Cattle, with or without Carriages, and for Foot Passengers', and the enterprise was constituted as 'One Body Politick and Corporate by the Name and Style of the Thames Archway Company'. The capital was £140,000. Vazie, the Mole, certainly fulfilled Charles Clarke's requirements in producing greater 'profoundness of thought and depths of professional talent'. These preliminary operations were sound enough but it is difficult in hindsight to see how he persuaded so many supporters that the building of the tunnel itself was a practical proposition. He was a practical man himself, however, and he brought with him a team of fellow Cornish miners to work on the job.

He started by sinking a shaft near Lavender Lane, Rotherhithe, some 330 feet back from the river's bank. From the base of the shaft he proposed to drive a timber driftway beneath the river to connect with another shaft sunk on the north bank. The driftway was to be a miner's passage only about 5 feet high with just enough room for two men to pass each other. Its construction and the maintenance of the timber called for all the skill of these experienced Cornish miners. Once the driftway had been completed as a pilot tunnel it was to serve as a drain for the full size tunnel which would be built above it. What Vazie did not at any time explain was how this larger tunnel was to be driven across the river—a pioneer engineering project which nobody, apart from the semi-mythical engineers of Babylon, had attempted.

Though they had come forward without too much hesitation with their cash, the company directors acted from the outset with a good deal of caution and parsimony. When the Cornishmen sank their shaft some 35 feet below Rotherhithe they ran into water-soaked gravel and a quicksand. Vazie had foreseen this possibility and had requested a 50 horse-power steam engine for pumping but the directors had ruled this out as an extravagance and authorized a 14 horse-power engine, which was quite inadequate. When the shaft reached a depth of just over 40 feet therefore the pumps were overwhelmed and work was brought to a standstill. Vazie had spent £7,000 of the company's money and the directors seemed inclined to cut their losses. Fortunately, however, more investors came in, upon one of the major shareholders taking responsibility for the cost of finishing the shaft. With a reduced diameter the shaft was then carried down to a depth of 76 feet below Trinity High Water. The cost had again exceeded all estimates and the directors passed a resolution: 'To suspend the works relating to the driftway until the opinion of a professional man of eminence has been taken on the various matters respecting it.' Once again John Rennie was called in, with William Chapman, a well-known canal engineer, as fellow consultant. The advice they offered was contradictory and negative. While Vazie continued to cool his heels the board turned to a third consultant, Davies Giddy (who later changed his name to Gilbert), who was a prominent Cornish Member of Parliament and later became President of the Royal Society. More significantly he was a confidant and friend of Richard Trevithick. He wrote this account of their relationship:

> About the year 1796 I remember learning from Mr Jonathan Hornblower that a Tall & strong young man had made his

appearance among Engineers, and that on more than one occasion he had threatened some people who contradicted him, to fling them into the Engine Shaft.

In the latter part of November of that year I was called to London as a Witness in a Steam Engine Case.... There I believe that I first saw Mr Richard Trevithick, Junr., and certainly there I first became acquainted with him.

Our correspondence commenced soon afterwards, and he was very frequently in the habit of calling at Tredrea to ask my opinion on various Projects that occur'd to his mind—some of them very ingenious, and others so wild as not to rest on any foundation at all.

In the case of the proposed tunnel the boot was on the other foot, for Giddy recommended Richard Trevithick to work on the project.

Trevithick in a letter to Giddy dated 'Limehouse, 1807, Aug. 11th.' confirmed with characteristic spelling his taking of the job:

Last monday [i.e. Aug. 10th] I closed with the Tunnel gents. I have agreed with them to give them advice and conduct the Driveing the level through to the opposite side, as was proposed when you attended the commette; to receive £500 when the Drift is halfway through, and £500 more when its holed on the opposite side. I have wrote to Cornwall for more men for them. Its intended to put 3 men in each core [of] six hours' course. I think this will be making a thousand pounds very easey, and withoute any risque of a loss on my side, and as I must be allways near the spot to attend to the engines on the river, an hour's attendance every day on the tunnel will be of little or no inconvenience to me. [I] hope 9 months will compleat it. From the recommendation you gave me, they are in great hopes that the job will now be accomplishd; and as far as Capn Hodge and my self culd judg from the ground in the bottom of the pit, theres no dought of compleating it speedily. I am very much obliged to you for throwing this job in my way, and shall strickley attend to it, both for our credit as well as my own profit.

So Richard Trevithick, 6 feet 2 inches tall, self-educated, former wrestler and weight-lifter, took charge of the enterprise with the disgruntled fellow Cornishman, Vazie, as assistant and with new miners brought up from Cornwall. They used traditional mining methods to keep earth from caving in by sheathing the walls and roof with timbers. A new 30 horse-power steam engine installed at the bottom of the shaft worked pumps, provided a primitive ventilating system and later was also used to pull loaded wagons from the face of the excavation. Somehow three men managed to work in the confined space, in six-hour shifts, crouching or kneeling, breathing stale air, soaked by the water that dripped incessantly. Only for a couple of months did Vazie and Trevithick manage to tolerate one another. Then in October 1807, by which time the drift had extended to nearly 400 feet, Robert Vazie was dismissed from his position as resident engineer, which he had held for four and a half years, during which time he said he had not slept one night away from the work. Among the directors of the company he left a number of sympathizers, who took every opportunity to decry Trevithick's subsequent activities.

The Cornish giant in fact was frequently at war with individual directors or with the company as a whole, though nobody could deny his single-mindedness in his pursuit of the work. His letters to Giddy were a safety-valve. At the beginning of January 1808, for instance, he wrote:

It was strongley proposd by one of the proprietors when the drift was half-way in to open from that place the tunnel to 16 ft high & 16 ft wide. I refusd to do it, knowing [that] this water and quick sand was over our head, and that as soon as we began to incline the bottom of the Drift to the surface on the north side we shod be into it. It was with the greatest difficulty that we culd stop it in the drift, onely 2½ ft wide and 5 ft high, and if we had opened the Tunnel to the full size, every man that might have been underground at the time must have been lost, and the river through to the Tunnel in 10 Minutes, for the water wod have brought the 2½ ft stratum of quick sand into the Tunnel, and then the clay roofe wod have sunk under the weight of the river; for it wod have been impossible to have stopd it in to 16 ft high & 16 ft wide; and the engine would have been dround in one minute, and the sand wod have constaintly com away under water untill the roofe fell through to the river. This properitor have been very much exasperated against me ever since, because I wod not open the tunnel from the middle of the drift up to the full size. This gent was never in a mine in his life, neither do he know any thing about it. He calld a general meeting to disscharge me, but he was taken no notice of, and the thanks of the meeting given to me for my

good conduct, and his friend Mr Vaize disscharged. They have
offered me £1250 more for my attendance to open the Drift up to
the full size of the Tunnel, and wish me to engage with them
immidtly, before the first contract expires.

His single-mindedness in concentrating on the job had left its
mark on his domestic life. His visits to his family home at Cam-
borne in Cornwall had become less and less frequent, but the new
financial arrangement enabled him to persuade his wife Jane to
bring the family to London. His son later described the domestic
situation which landed Jane Trevithick and her family in a dingy
house near the mouth of the driftway.

There had been much correspondence about the wisdom of this
move. Mrs Trevithick's brother, Mr Henry Harvey, advised her
not to leave her home and friends, until things were more settled
and more certain in London. Trevithick's notes to his wife,
however, made everything easy and agreeable. More than 300
miles had to be travelled in a post-chaise occupied by herself and
her four little ones; the youngest of them a baby. The contrast
between her clean and fresh Cornish home and the habitation at
Rotherhithe did not help to remove the fatigue of the journey, and
a further disappointment awaited her. In her husband's pockets
were two of her last letters unopened. What reasons could possibly
be offered for such hard-hearted ingratitude? Trevithick's answer
to the charge was simply, 'You know, Jane, that your notes were
full of reasons for not coming to London, and I had not the heart
to read any more of them.'

The lack of amenities in Rotherhithe might have been more
tolerable if Jane had not had so much anxiety about the work
below ground. Toward the end of January 1808, soon after she
had been installed, Trevithick was standing with a miner who was
swinging his pick at the face of the excavation almost one thousand
feet from the tunnel entrance when there was a sudden inrush of
quicksand followed by a torrent of water. The two men turned
and ran. Half swimming, half staggering, they groped along the
darkened tunnel. The overtaking water reached their shoulders.
During their last minutes in the driftway they had to tip back
their heads and press their faces close to the ceiling to breathe.
Trevithick emerged from the flooded tunnel and dragged himself

shoeless and covered with mud through the streets to his home. Jane of course begged him to give up but he, characteristically, could only think of plans for stopping up the hole in the tunnel. Within a week the crater over the head of the excavation, at that time within 150 feet of the north bank of the river, was filled in with clay dropped in bags from a boat and Trevithick was writing to Giddy: 'if we have no farther delays we shall hole up to the surface in 10 or 12 days.'

By the time Giddy received that letter, however, the river had flooded in again and Trevithick was resorting to clay bags as before. This time the directors of the company lost heart, held an emergency meeting at Limehouse and ordered a stoppage of the work. Trevithick told them that the driftway could be completed only from above by excavating the bed of the river from within a series of coffer-dams and then laying a sectional cast-iron tunnel. The partisans of Robert Vazie were still against him, however, and there was a general lack of confidence. The dissatisfaction of them went to extraordinary lengths in laying a complaint before the Lord Mayor that the navigation of the river was being impeded by the heap of clay being laid over the hole, and in March 1808 the Thames Water Bailiff ordered all work on the river bed above the driftway to be halted.

When the company retained two eminent North Country engineers to report on Trevithick's work they upheld the competence of the Cornish giant in these words: 'He has shown most extraordinary skill and ingenuity in passing the quicksand; and we do not know any practical miner that we think more competent to the task than he is. We judge from the work itself, and until this occasion of viewing the work, we did not know Mr. Trevithick.'

But the directors remained faint-hearted. They made a public announcement offering a prize of £500 for anyone who would come forward with a scheme for completing the work. They appointed the mathematician Dr Charles Hutton and William Jessop, an eminent civil engineer, to act as judges. Hundreds of entries came from the general public: some forty of them could be taken seriously. In due course the judges reported: 'Though we cannot presume to set limits to the ingenuity of other men, we must confess that, under the circumstances which have been so clearly represented to us, we consider that an underground tunnel, which would be useful to the public and beneficial to the adventurers, is *impracticable*.' In the face of this, the Thames Archway Company went out of business.

Jane Trevithick left Limehouse with much relief and Richard Trevithick went on to many other exciting things in Britain and the New World. That very summer (1808) a steam engine of his was exciting *The Observer*. 'The most astonishing machine ever invented is a steam engine with four wheels so constructed that she will with ease and without any other aid, gallop from 15 to 20 miles an hour on any circle. She weighs 8 tons and is matched for the next Newmarket meeting against three horses to run 24 hours starting the same time.'

For men like Richard Trevithick these were lively times.

10

Tunnels Achieved

Trevithick's work, which so nearly cost him his life, vanished without a trace, but within a couple of decades another tunnel was beginning which nearly killed another great engineer, the younger Brunel, but survives to the present day. The Thames had defeated the Cornish engineers because they had not been able to devise the right equipment even in that century of prolific invention. Marc Isambard, the elder Brunel, discovered the right tool as a result of his rapacious curiosity. He never went anywhere without equipping himself with every small means of pursuing it —for instance a magnifying glass in his waistcoat pocket. In Chatham Dockyard superintending some extensive works, which included a small underground tunnel for the conveyance of timber from the Medway, he observed a piece of keel timber newly removed from a ship. It had been punctured by a ship-worm known as *teredo navalis*, a greater enemy to British shipping than hostile cannon. With his magnifying glass Brunel studied the action of a living worm digging into the wood with two razor-sharp shells. The mollusc then grinds the wood into a nourishing flour which is its diet, and this is excreted to form the lining of a smooth tunnel in which the creature works. It is protected at its head by the strong boring shells and from the sides by the tunnel lining of its own manufacture. Brunel's idea was to reproduce the mechanism of a ship-worm in iron—an iron cylinder propelled forward horizontally by jacks, enclosing miners working a cutting edge, with more miners behind them lining the excavation with bricks in quick-drying mortar. He took out his first patent for this in 1818 and modified it in ensuing years until it became known as his Great Shield. Brunel then came to regard the penetration of a tunnel beneath the Thames tideway as his personal destiny, and incidentally his hope of making the fortune which was always eluding him. He wrote: 'We may soon anticipate a speedy and total change in the face of the maps of this great metropolis—in that portion of it which has hitherto presented nothing but swampy desert—namely the parish of Rotherhithe. . . . This parish will soon display a scene of activity that is not to be witnessed anywhere else.'

A characteristic of Brunel which he shared with so many of the pioneers of his century, including his own son, was not only possession of immense self-confidence but ability to work and think at all levels. At no time in the planning of his tunnel did Brunel call upon the technical skills and resources of others. He had only his son as his assistant. He was just as self-assured when it came to raising the money and organizing a company and administration. He cheerfully accepted the need to become a lobbyist as well as an inventor. In 1823 with the aid of pamphlets, personal visits and meetings he was canvassing businessmen, bankers and directors of canal companies. Early in the following year he had succeeded in arousing enough enthusiasm for a public meeting of well-wishers to subscribe shares, and within three days nearly £180,000 had been promised. Before forming his company Brunel, leaving no stone unturned, visited the Iron Duke: 'Waited on the Duke of Wellington by appointment, the object of which was to have the plan of the mode of proceeding with the tunnel explained to him. His Grace made many very good observations and raised great objections; but after having explained to him my Plan and the expedients I had in reserve, His Grace appeared to be satisfied and to be disposed to subscribe.'

So the Thames Tunnel Company was formed in 1824, with powers defined by Act of Parliament for 'Making and Maintaining a Tunnel under the Thames . . . from some place in the parish of St John of Wapping in the County of Middlesex to the opposite shore of the said river in the parish of St Mary, Rotherhithe, in the County of Surrey, with sufficient approaches thereto.' Four thousand £50 shares were offered to the public, making a capital sum which was less than Brunel had estimated, but Brunel was appointed chief engineer on a three-year contract with separate payments for the use of his Shield patent.

The company was given the power to erect turnpikes at either end of the completed tunnel, and to charge the following tolls:

Foot passengers	2*d*
Six-horse carriages	2 6*d*
Three- or four-horse carriages	2 0*d*
Two-horse carriages	1 0*d*
One-horse carriages	6*d*
Horse-drawn wagons and carts	4*d*
Wheelbarrows	2½*d*
Horses, mules or asses without carts	2*d*
Not more than 1/0*d* for every score of cattle	
Not more than 6*d* for every score of calves, sheep or lambs	
Not more than 6*d* for every score of geese, ducks or turkeys.	

Cow Court, Rotherhithe, a site 140 feet back from the south bank of the river, was chosen for the headquarters. The line of the tunnel was to be three-quarters of a mile upstream from Vazie's drift. Jolliffe and Banks, with the experience of their work on Rennie's new London Bridge, were retained to make test borings along the line of the tunnel. The beginning of work at Cow Court in March 1825 became a public event. The bells of St Mary's, Rotherhithe, pealed through the opening day. Flags fluttered and streams of carriages arrived. The focus of attention in the middle of the yard was a great iron hoop weighing 25 tons, the foundation of a 42-foot tower which was to be the entry shaft of the tunnel. As the bands played Brunel laid the first brick of his shaft with a silver trowel, and his seventeen-year-old son Isambard, whose fame was to exceed his, laid the second brick. As the shaft was sunk there was a constant stream of famous visitors, including the Duke of Wellington, Robert Peel and Prince Lieven. The gentlemen of all nationalities used the workmen's ladder to enter the shaft; for the ladies Brunel rigged up a well-upholstered chair on ropes. After four months one of the workmen, the worse for drink, fell down the shaft and was killed. He was the first of many casualties. When the shaft was 63 feet below the surface the digging of the tunnel began and for the remainder of 1825 progress was relatively safe. The following year the tunnellers struck a patch of loose wet gravel and quicksand and the pumps had to work harder. What was more alarming was the firedamp which began to enter the tunnel. This carburetted hydrogen would ignite in the already contaminated air, causing flames to spurt. It was at its worst at high tide, when bursts of flame would make the cells of the shield unbearably hot, so that water sizzled when it dropped on the cast-iron. Flashes even singed the hair of the workmen, and there were many cases of what were called tunnel sickness. The day-to-day effects of the gas on Brunel himself were noted in his diary at a later stage in 1838:

14th May. . . . The gas has been extremely offensive this morning and ever since.

16th May. . . . Inflammable gas. Men complaining very much. . . . Mason. . . . is in good spirits, but Francis is very bad.

17th May. . . . It appears that there is a greater number of disabled men than at any other time before. I felt very much weakened by the inspection I made of the shield.

26th May. . . . Heywood (a miner) died this morning. Two more on the sick list. Page is evidently sinking very fast. . . . I inspected the shield. Not much water there, but the air excessively offensive. . . . It affects the eyes. I feel much debility after having been some time below. My sight is rather dim today. All complain of pain in the eyes. Dixon (another of the assistant engineers) has reported that twice in one shift he was completely depossessed of sight for some time.

27th May. . . . My eyes very dim and both bloodshot. Page very much affected today. Almost all day laying down on his sopha complaining much. . . .

28th May. Wood, a bricklayer, fell senseless in the top floor. The assistants complain, being affected in different ways.

29th May. Short came to the office and reported himself unable to work. Affected like Huggins and all others. A most efficient and intrepid man. Bowyer died today or yesterday. A good man. . . .

30th May. This night, viz, about 10 o'clock, walking as I did up and down the arches which are lighted enough to give an extensive view of the work, I could not refrain from the reflection that the brave men who are the agents for the execution of a work like this

are so many men that are sacrificed and my assistants likewise—
that in a few weeks most probably, they will be lingering under
the influence of a slow and insidious poison.
1st June. . . . Found that Harman (a miner) is very much affected
like the others, that his spirits are much depressed, so is the same
of others from the influence of the gases.
4th June. Sullivan: Sent him to the hospital, he being almost
blind. . . . The best men are very much affected. Influx continues
moderate and regular. . . . On my return . . . to the office I was
just in time to support poor Page who had just fainted. Dr Mur-
dock was sent for. He is in a very bad way. All over with him I am
persuaded.

The tunnel, which was 1,200 feet long, with interruptions, took
eighteen years and twenty-three days to build. Such diary entries
as this reflect the many hazards encountered and casualties
suffered between 1825 and 1843. The astonishing aspect of the
enterprise was that it went on as it began, as a public spectacle.
Even when disaster threatened, even when work had to cease
altogether through lack of money, famous men from all walks of
life and from many nations received what would now be called
VIP treatment at the workings, while the general public in their
thousands paid to see one of the wonders of the age and to walk
beneath the waters of the Thames. More than a thousand people
paid to see the tunnel during the first three days it was open to
the public. Even when work on the tunnel ceased for nearly seven
years there was always a steady trickle of visitors, providing a
small income. Public interest indeed never flagged during those
long years while the tunnel progressed by fits and starts and was
christened by *The Times* as 'The Great Bore'. The Bore pun was
also taken up by the poet Thomas Hood in his *Ode to M. Brunel*,
which appeared at a time when financial difficulties had so beset
the Thames Tunnel Company that work had ceased and the
future of the project was a matter for speculation.

> I'll tell thee with thy tunnel what to do;
> Light up thy boxes, build a bin or two,
> The wine does better than such water trades,
> Stick up a sign, the sign of the Bore's head;
> I've drawn it ready for thee in black lead,
> And make thy cellar subterranean—thy Shades!

Alas! half-way thou hadst proceeded, when
Old Thames, through roof, not water-proof,
Came, 'like a tide in the affairs of men';
And with a mighty stormy kind of roar,
Reproachful of thy wrong,
Burst out in that old song,
Of Incledon's, beginning, 'Cease, rude Bore—'.
Other great speculations have been nursed,
Till want of proceeds laid them on a shelf;
But thy concern was at the worst
When it began to liquidate itself!

Well! Monsieur Brunel,
How prospers now thy mighty undertaking,
To join by a hollow way the Bankside friends
Of Rotherhithe and Wapping,
Never be stopping;
But poking, groping, in the dark keep making
An archway, underneath the dabs and gudgeons,
For colliermen and pitchy old curmudgeons,
To cross the water in inverse proportion,
Walk under steam-boats, under the keel's ridge,
To keep down all extortion,
And with sculls to diddle London Bridge!
In a fresh hut a great new bore to worry,
Thou didst to earth thy human terrier follow,
Hopeful at last, from Middlesex to Surrey,
To give us the 'view hollow'.

This of course was addressed to the elder Brunel, for whom the
construction of the tunnel was the major triumph of an inventive
lifetime, the culmination of which, prolonged by delays which
nearly killed him, was the receipt of a knighthood from Queen
Victoria. Though the invention and promotion of the tunnel
belonged to the elder Brunel, the main burden of the supervision of the practical work fell upon his famous son, Isambard,
and it is his diary entries which most vividly depict the prolonged
stress and frustration of this first ever tunnel under a river. He was
only eighteen years old when he was first employed in a super-
visory capacity. He celebrated his coming-of-age with a concert
given in the tunnel on 11th April 1827. It was the year when the
river made its first eruption into the workings.

A few days before the first flooding Isambard wrote in his
diary: 'Notwithstanding every prudence on our part, a disaster

may still occur—*may it not be when the arch is full of visitors!* It is too awful to think of it. I have done my part by recommending to the directors to shut the tunnel. . . .' There were no visitors in the tunnel when the flood came a few days later. Brunel just managed to escape with his life after heroically rescuing others. On the Sunday following the parson at Rotherhithe church in his sermon declared that the inundation was 'a just judgement on the presumptuous aspirations of mortal men. . . .' Nevertheless young Brunel wasted no time in attacking the disaster. He borrowed a diving-bell from the West India Dock Company in order himself to go down and inspect the hole in the bed of the river. He also took a boat down inside the workings to inspect the flood in the tunnel. In his journal this extraordinary young man described these two operations:

'What a dream it now appears to me! Going down in the diving bell, finding and examining the hole! The novelty of the thing, the excitement of the occasional risk attending our submarine (aquatic) excursions, the crowds of boats to witness our works all amused—the anxious watching of the shaft—seeing it full of water, rising and falling with the tide with the most provoking regularity —at last, by dint of clay bags, clay and gravel, a perceptible difference. We then began pumping, at last reaching the crown of the arch—what sensations! . . .

I must make some little indian ink sketches of our boat excursions to the frames: the low, dark, gloomy, cold arch; the heap of earth almost up to the crown, hiding the frames and rendering it quite uncertain what state they were in and what might happen; the hollow rushing of water; the total darkness of all around rendered distinct by the glimmering light of a candle or two, carried by ourselves; crawling along the bank of earth, a dark recess at the end—quite dark—water rushing from it in such quantities as to render it uncertain whether the ground was secure; at last reaching the frames—choked up to the middle rail of the top box—frames evidently leaning back and sideways considerably—staves in curious directions, bags and chisel rods protruding in all directions; reaching No. 12, the bags apparently without support and swelling into the frame threaten every minute to close inside brickwork. All bags—a cavern, *huge, misshapen* with water— a cataract coming from it—candles going out. . . .

Incredibly, distinguished sightseers continued to arrive and even to participate. One of these was Charles Bonaparte who was

accompanied by the geologist, Sir Roderick Murchison, who left
his own hilarious account of the visit.

> The first operation we underwent (one which I never repeated)
> was to go down in a diving-bell upon the cavity by which the
> Thames had broken in. Buckland and Featherstonehaugh, having
> been the first to volunteer, came up with such red faces and such
> staring eyes, that I felt no great inclination to follow their example,
> particularly as Charles Bonaparte was most anxious to avoid the
> dilemma, excusing himself by saying that his family were very
> short-necked and subject to apoplexy, etc; but it would not do to
> show the white feather; I got in, and induced him to follow me.
> The effect was, as I expected, most oppressive, and then on the
> bottom what did we see but dirty gravel and mud, from which I
> brought up a fragment of one of Hunt's blacking bottles. We
> soon pulled the string, and were delighted to breathe the fresh air.
>   The first folly was, however, quite overpowered by the next.
> We went down the shaft on the south bank, and got, with young
> Brunel, into a punt, which he was to steer into the tunnel till we
> reached the repairing shield. About eleven feet of water were still
> in the tunnel, leaving just space enough above our heads for Brunel
> to stand up and claw the ceiling and sides to impel us. As we were
> proceeding he called out, 'Now, gentlemen, if by accident there
> should be a rush of water, I shall turn the punt over and prevent
> you being jammed against the roof, and we shall then be carried
> out and up the shaft!' On this C. Bonaparte remarked, 'But I
> cannot swim!' and, just as he had said the words, Brunel, swing-
> ing carelessly from right to left, fell overboard, and out went the
> candles with which he was lighting up the place. Taking this for
> the *sauve qui peut*, fat C.B., then the very image of Napoleon at St
> Helena, was about to roll after him, when I held him fast, and, by
> the glimmering light from the entrance, we found young Brunel,
> who swam like a fish, coming up on the other side of the punt, and
> soon got him on board. We of course called out for an immediate
> retreat, for really there could not be a more foolhardy and
> ridiculous risk of our lives, inasmuch as it was just the moment of
> trial as to whether the Thames would make a further inroad or not.

The fact that there was an element of foolhardiness in such
tunnel excursions was proved a few days later when two of the
directors of the tunnel company insisted on inspecting the works
with Brunel and an escort of miners. A Mr Martin, one of the
directors, suddenly stood up in the boat and struck his head
against the roof of the tunnel. He fell backwards against the others,

capsizing the craft. There was a desperate struggle in the water. The foolhardy Martin, who was a non-swimmer like most of the party, was rescued with the rest, but one of the miners was drowned.

The drama of the tunnel was celebrated in the West End of London with a theatrical spectacle entitled: *The Thames Tunnell*; *or Harlequin Excavator*. Characters in this pantomime included Father Thames, Ancient Flounder, a Thames Eel and a Thames Waterman, whose ditty claimed him to be 'an enemy to bridges above the tunnels below the Thames'. A broadsheet advertising the show promised a 'subaqueous Grotto beneath the Source of the Thames, View on the River Bank near Rotherhithe, the Interior of the Thames Tunnell with its Curious Machinery', and the action included the re-enactment of the flooding with a replica of Brunel's Shield being swept away.

The archways were nearly 550 feet long when tunnelling began again in 1827. Optimism rose and had to be kept up. Like so many nineteenth-century pioneers—and De Lesseps springs to mind— the Brunels were adept at showmanship and public relations. The work in the tunnel had been going for only just two months when they arranged a banquet in the tunnel. No theatrical extravaganza above ground was a match for this bizarre event staged to celebrate the triumph of man's ingenuity over natural forces. The archways were hung with crimson drape and decorated with candelabra from the Portable Gas Company. In the western archway of the tunnel a table was laid with a white cloth for forty distinguished guests. In the adjoining arch was an even larger table prepared less extravagantly for the one hundred and twenty miners, bricklayers and workmen on the job. The elder Brunel stayed away in order to project the image of Isambard as his successor.

So it was the young Brunel who welcomed the distinguished guests to the music of the uniformed band of the Coldstream Guards. There was a succession of toasts. They culminated when Mr Bandinel of the Foreign Office, announcing the victory of the British Navy commanded by Admiral Codrington (a supporter of Brunel) over the Turkish fleet at Navarino, thus liberating the Greeks and avenging Byron's death, declared 'the Turkish power has received a severer check than it has ever suffered since Mahomed drew the sword. It may be said that the wine-abjuring Prophet conquered by water—upon that element his successors have now been signally defeated. My motto, therefore, on this occasion, when we meet to celebrate the expulsion of the river from this spot is—Down with water and Mahomed—wine and Codrington forever!'

Finally the ceremonious occasion was rounded off by the leader of the workpeople presenting the young resident engineer with a pickaxe and shovel as symbols of their trade.

The triumph did not last. After seeing in the New Year in the tunnel the resident engineer was again fighting for his life toward the middle of January 1828 when the river broke in again. This second inundation caused the seven-year suspension of work and put I. K. Brunel on his sickbed, from which he wrote:

I have now been laid up quite useless for 14 weeks and upwards, ever since the 14th January. I shan't forget that day in a hurry, very near finished my journey then; when the danger is over, it is rather amusing than otherwise—while it existed I can't say the feeling was at all uncomfortable. If I was to say the contrary, I should be nearer the truth in this instance. While exertions could still be made and hope remained of stopping the ground it was an excitement which has always been a luxury to me. When we were obliged to run, I felt nothing in particular; I was only thinking of the best way of getting us on and the probable state of the arches. When knocked down, I certainly gave myself up, but I took it very much as a matter of course, which I had expected the moment we quitted the frames, for I never expected we should get out. The instant I disengaged myself and got breath again—all dark—I bolted into the other arch—this saved me by laying hold of the railrope—the engine *must* have stopped a minute. I stood still nearly a minute. I was anxious for poor Ball and Collins, who I felt too sure had never risen from the fall we had all had and were, as I thought, *crushed* under the great stage. I kept calling them by name to encourage them and make them also (if still able) come through the opening. While standing there the effect was—*grand*— the roar of the rushing water in a confined passage, and by its velocity rushing past the opening was grand, *very grand*. I cannot compare it to anything, cannon can be nothing to it. At last it came bursting through the opening. I was then obliged to be off—but up to that moment, as far as my sensations were concerned, and distinct from the idea of the loss of six poor fellows whose death I could not then foresee, kept there.

The seven years of suspense were caused by the inability of Marc Brunel and the company to raise further money. There was never suspension of hope, and to the sightseeing public at least there was a continued maintenance of confidence, for the end of the workings was sealed off and covered by a great mirror, and people continued to pay for the privilege of encountering one of the engineering wonders of the age and walking beneath the river. Young Brunel allowed an element of facetiousness to temper his despair. 'The young Rennies, whatever their real merit, will have built London Bridge, the finest bridge in Europe, and have such a connection with government as to defy competition. Palmer has built new London Docks and thus without labour has established a connection which ensures his fortune, while I—shall have been engaged on the Tunnel which failed, which was abandoned—a pretty recommendation. . . .

'I'll turn misanthrope, get a huge Meerschaum, as big as myself and smoke away melancholy—and yet that can't be done without money and that can't be got without working for it. Dear me, what a world this is where starvation itself is an expensive luxury. But damn all croaking, the Tunnel must go on, it shall go on. . . .'

With the aid of the Treasury the tunnel went on in March 1835. The river continued to flood the enterprise in August and November 1837 and in March 1838.

In June 1840 the Brunels took possession of a site for the Wapping shaft. In March 1843 *The Times* reported the start of the great opening ceremony in these words: 'The ceremony of throwing open this "great bore" to the public was performed on Saturday last under favour of good-natured old Father Thames. The grand rendezvous was the Rotherhithe shaft on the Surrey side of the river, where two marquees had been erected, one for the accommodation of the directors and proprietors with their friends, and the other for the reception of visitors. The hoisting of flags and the ringing of bells naturally drew a great crowd of idlers to the spot at an early hour of the day. . . .'

Fifty thousand people paid their pennies and went through

within twenty-seven hours of the official opening. Within fifteen weeks the millionth traveller had passed the turnstiles. In July Queen Victoria arrived in the royal barge at the tunnel pier and walked the length of the tunnel for which she awarded Marc Brunel his knighthood. Like her subjects she had to climb up and down the sweeps of stairs from the ground level and to traverse the tunnel on foot. The scheme for vehicular traffic to pass through the tunnel had not materialized—and it never would.

To celebrate the first anniversary of its opening a three-day fair was held in the tunnel and more than 66,000 people attended. Its value as a means of crossing the river, however, was clearly a disappointment. Nothing had been done about ramps for vehicular traffic and by the end of that first year it was becoming evident that the tunnel was not a commercial success apart from its potential as a showpiece. The 'grand fancy fairs' continued but by 1849 there was no dividend. The attractions in the tunnel, which included steam music, glass-blowing demonstrations, weight-lifting and electrical gadgetry, with fresco paintings and innumerable stalls, continued right through to 1851 when the Great Exhibition in Hyde Park was at its height. In the month of August that year in fact twice as many people went through the tunnel as visited the Crystal Palace in Hyde Park but after a time the tunnel acquired a bad reputation, like the first Westminster Bridge, as a haunt of prostitution. When Nathaniel Hawthorne saw it in 1855 he was daunted:

> The entrance to the Thames Tunnel is beneath a large circular building, which is lighted from the top, so as to throw the daylight into the great depth to which we descend, by a winding staircase, before reaching the level of the bore. A road must commence, I should think, at least a mile off on either side of the river, in order to make it possible for vehicles to go through the tunnel; so great is the descent. On reaching the bottom, we saw a closed door, which we opened, and passing through it, found ourselves in the Tunnel—an arched corridor, of apparently interminable length, gloomily lighted with jets of gas at regular intervals—plastered at the sides, and stone beneath the feet. It would have made an admirable prison. . . . There are people who spend their lives here, seldom or never, I presume, seeing any daylight; except perhaps a little in the morning. All along the extent of this corridor, in little

alcoves, there are stalls or shops, kept principally by women, who, as you approach, are seen through the dusk, offering for sale views of the Tunnel, put up, with a little magnifying glass, in cases of Derbyshire spar; also, cheap jewelry and multifarious trumpery; also cakes, candy, ginger-beer, and such small refreshments. There was one shop that must, I think, have opened into the other corridor of the Tunnel, so capacious it seemed; and here were dioramic views of various cities and scenes of the daylight-world, all shown by gas, while the Thames rolled its tide and its shipping over our heads. So far as any present use is concerned, the Tunnel is an entire failure, and labor and immensity of money thrown away. I did not meet or pass above half a dozen passengers through its whole extent; whereas, no doubt, it would require a continual swarm, like that on London Bridge, besides horsemen, carts, carriages of all sorts, to pay anything like the interest of the money. Perhaps in coming ages, the approaches to the Tunnel will be obliterated, its corridors choked up with mud, its precise locality unknown, and nothing be left of it but an obscure tradition. . . .

Hawthorne's gloomy forecast did not take into account the railway possibilities. In 1862 when the company's funds were down to twenty pounds, though the tunnel structurally was still in perfect condition, negotiations started. Two years later an agreement was signed with the East London Railway Company, which paid £200,000 for the tunnel. The first trains steamed beneath the Thames in 1870. They were electrified in 1918, the tunnel by that time being a part of the London Underground system. It remains in use, and the journey between Rotherhithe and Wapping takes less than a minute in this most easterly railway crossing of the tideway. When Wapping Station was rebuilt after being bombed in the Second World War, a modern slate plaque was placed there. It states: 'The tunnel which runs under the Thames from this station was the first tunnel for public traffic ever to be driven beneath a river.'

In October 1869 the *Illustrated London News* announced: 'While the work of converting Sir Isambard Brunel's Thames Tunnel, from Wapping to Rotherhithe, to the use of a railway, is still going on in silence, a second tunnel, crossing beneath the river from Tower-hill to Tooley-street, near the London Bridge railway station, has been constructed in the present year.' This was the

work of Peter William Barlow (1809–85), a civil engineer who had
already been associated with Thames bridge and with railway
development, and Henry Greathead, the contractor who gave his
name to the Greathead Shield, which seems to have been a joint
invention of the two men. They were retained by a company
formed to promote what could be said to have been London's first
tube, though the first tube railway in the full sense of the word did
not begin to operate until twenty years later. The Tower Subway,
which still exists as a kind of ghost tunnel, was planned as a swift
mechanical means of taking people across the river. Instead of
brick it was lined with cast-iron, having an interior diameter of
only about 7 feet. 'This circular tunnel is not intended for foot-
passenger traffic,' wrote the *Illustrated London News*.

> It is meant for a tramway of 2 ft 6 in gauge, on which is to run a
> light iron omnibus of 10½ ft long, 5 ft 3 in wide, and 5 ft 11 in
> high. This will accommodate fourteen people with the most per-
> fect ease. Ordinary lifts will take them down and up the shafts at
> each end, and at the end of the shaft the 'bus' will be waiting.
> For the first hundred feet or so the omnibus will be pulled up a
> rope fixed to a stationary engine; after that it will descend by its
> own velocity down the incline and up the incline on the other side
> to the foot of the shaft. The whole transit, including time for
> descent and ascent, is not to exceed three minutes.

The omnibus was made of iron 'light, but very strong, and runs
upon eight wheels'. There was a waiting room for passengers at
the foot of each of the vertical shafts. The work was efficiently and
quickly carried through between the years 1869 and 1870, when
the *Illustrated London News* again enthused, emphasizing the virtues
of speed which the new project would bring to London life.

> The descent of the shaft occupies twenty-five seconds, and the
> omnibus journey seventy seconds; so that a passenger may descend
> into the shaft at Tower-hill and emerge in Vine-street in a minute
> and three-quarters from the time of his descent. Allowing for all
> ordinary causes of detention—such as missing the lift at the
> moment of its descent, or being just too late for the omnibus—the
> journey from point to point cannot occupy more than five minutes.
> The lifts, as they only carry half as many passengers as the
> omnibus, will make twice as many journeys; and it is intended to
> give priority to first-class passengers, who pay twopence, while the
> second-class passengers pay one penny.

Walter Thornbury, writing in a popular miscellany called *Old and New London*, mentioned wider implications: 'The gain to the East-end of London by this successful and cleverly executed undertaking is enormous, and the intercourse between the north and south banks of the Thames is greatly facilitated; and the conception has been seized upon by Mr. Bateman as the basis of his well-known suggestion for a submarine tube to carry a railway from England to France.'

In fact the cable railway and its engines, which also ran the lifts, very soon vanished from the subaqueous scene. Several reporters had mentioned with relish that when the omnibus was stationary in mid tunnel it was possible to hear the paddles of ships passing overhead, and it may well have been that too many passengers had this experience too often. Charles Welch, writing in 1894, mentioned that the omnibus was withdrawn 'in consequence of several accidents'.

For many years the tunnel lingered on for the benefit of foot passengers. Welch stated: 'in spite of the charge of one half-penny for toll, nearly one million passengers a year are estimated to cross the river by means of the subway.' Toward the end of its public service, before it was made redundant by the opening of the Tower Bridge, it was clearly one of the least attractive crossings of the river. The recollection of a Mr Morris of Hastings was reported in the *Guardian* in 1965: 'I was only a lad paying visits to the City Tea Warehouses in 1884, obtaining samples from the latest tea imports later to be blended by tea tasters. There was a wharf (Butler's) lying on the opposite side of the river with two routes of getting there, one by private ferry which might delay me an hour or more before the boatman could get a sufficient number; the other route was through a dismal frightening tunnel. The entrance on Tower Hill looked somewhat like a kiosk. The worn out spiral stairs went down to the bottom of a long tunnel ... no more than six feet in diameter, ill-lighted with water trickling down and a constant noise of the water above. I certainly hesitated when I reached the bottom of the spiral stairs, wondering whether I would get through at all. It was difficult to pass anyone coming in the opposite direction and very seldom I ever met anyone at all, perhaps a man would appear in the dim light. The payment at the end at the turnstile was a halfpenny. The alternative route was by ferry.'

The kiosk on Tower Hill was still standing in 1971 when these pages were written. It bears the legend 'The London Hydraulic Company 1869' and goes largely unnoticed, in competition with the Tower Yeoman and other attractions at the public entrance to the Tower of London. The tunnel has been in use for many years to carry a hydraulic pipeline for the servicing of elevators and cranes, which was the business of the London Hydraulic Company whose activities have now been taken over by others. From time to time experts descend the series of flights of rusty iron stairs to the bottom of the shafts in order to inspect or repair the pipelines in the tunnel. Those who go down into what is now a cramped passage beneath the tideway prefer not to linger; it is one of the loneliest places in London.

One result of the work of Barlow and Greathead in this sadly unsuccessful subway was the construction some twenty years later of London's first tube line, the City and South London Railway, which until a few months prior to its opening in December 1890 was known as the City of London and Southwark Subway. It ran from a terminus at the corner of King Arthur Street and King William Street for a distance of just over three miles to a station in Stockwell south of the river. The up and down lines passed under the Thames in separate tunnels, and on the south side of the river the tunnels ran beneath the public thoroughfare, a plan followed later by all tubes in inner London. Tickets were not issued; passengers paid at turnstiles, used hydraulic lifts or winding stairs and travelled in small carriages without windows, the trains being hauled by electric locomotives. The Prince of Wales (afterwards King Edward VII) performed the opening ceremony. When the tube system developed the old City and South London line and tunnel were incorporated in the London Bridge to Stockwell section of the Northern Line.

The engineer of the line was James Henry Greathead, whose tunnelling shield was used subsequently on all the London tube lines. Acting as consultant was Sir Benjamin Baker, who was to play an active part in London's tube railway construction dealt with in Chapter 14 (see p. 150).

11

Bazalgette and the Metropolitan
Board of Works

The present pattern of bridges, tunnels and ferries crossing the London tideway has changed very little from the seventies of the last century to this. Improvements and enlargements have been carried out here and there and more are somewhat urgently contemplated in the seventies of this century, but the planning efforts of the Victorians, at a time when town planning as we now know it had no official existence, moulded London in its relation to the river imaginatively and, as it has turned out, lastingly. The source of this was the Metropolitan Board of Works, which existed from 1855 to 1888, and more especially its chief engineer, Sir Joseph William Bazalgette (1819–91), whose modest memorial on the Embankment bears the legend FLUMINI VINCULA POSUIT, which could be translated that he placed the river in chains.

Bazalgette might better be described as a liberator, for in his capacity as engineer-in-chief to the Metropolitan Board of Works he was responsible for the first main drainage system in London and for the laying down of the Thames embankments. Sir Christopher Wren had proposed an embankment as part of the redevelopment of London after the Great Fire and this, had it not been swept aside because of the expenditure on other works, would no doubt have had a profound effect on river crossings in subsequent centuries.

Bazalgette started work on the Victoria Embankment in 1864, reclaiming nearly forty acres of mudbanks. The work cost nearly £1,200,000 and embodied the construction of the District Railway below ground and an important element of the sewage system. It was completed in 1870, a year after the Albert Embankment on the south bank of the river, which cost over £1,000,000 and saved a large part of Lambeth from periodic inundation. The third great work, the Chelsea Embankment, was finished in 1874.

The Metropolitan Board of Works was the first large-scale integration of local authority in London. At its death in 1888, accompanied by a large number of vague charges of corruption, it was superseded by a more democratically and better organized London County Council, which became the Greater London Council. Financially the Board derived its means from two sources—the rates and a part of the proceeds of coal and wine duties. This second source was traditional. The rebuilding of St Paul's and other works following the Great Fire, and the construction of the first Blackfriars Bridge, had been carried out with such aid, which was also enjoyed by the City Corporation for the purpose of large public improvements. From the 1860s to the 1880s the Board did not have to rely entirely on the rates it levied to carry out its enlightened programmes, but toward the end of its time the value of the contribution from coal and wine had dwindled. In 1888 the amount received was about £3,250 as compared with £1,075,000 from rates. Though the rates it levied were low enough by this century's standards the Board was constantly under suspicion. Only four years after its creation *The Times* was complaining: 'Unhappily, the Board spends our money and rates our property, and we cannot afford to let them alone to their own devices.'

Nevertheless it was the Metropolitan Board of Works—and Bazalgette—which first attempted to deal with the tideway as a whole in the interests of the public. For more than a century there had been growing agitation against tolls. In spite of the population explosion and the revolution in transport on road, rail and river, the crossings of the tideway had remained largely in private hands. When the Board was created in 1855 there were only three bridges in London over the Thames free of tolls—London and Blackfriars owned by the City Corporation and Westminster Bridge then in the charge of the Office of Works. The Board set about freeing the remaining bridges by an Act of Parliament passed in 1877 enabling it to purchase all the private interests concerned. Between 1878 and 1880 eleven bridges were made public highways free of toll at a cost of £1,400,000. In 1879, on Queen Victoria's birthday, 24th May, the Prince and Princess of Wales, afterwards King Edward VII and Queen Alexandra, spent a truly transpontine afternoon driving across Lambeth, Vauxhall, Chelsea, the Albert and Battersea Bridges to celebrate their liberation from tolls. With the successful rebuilding and refurbishing of a number of these crossings above London Bridge, one of the Board's problems was to tackle the lack of crossings below London Bridge, where commercial, industrial and dock enterprises had been consolidating since the early years of the century, bringing with them a population on both sides of the river estimated at the time to be about 1,700,000.

Bazalgette had made an intensive study of this. After the abolition of tolls the pressures for action increased, especially from ratepayers east of London Bridge. They had contributed toward the cost of toll abolition in the western reaches and naturally they were agitating for some comparable improvement in facilities on the lower tideway. The first attempt to meet this demand was a Bill proposing a scheme for a high-level bridge near the Tower. It was thrown out. In 1884 the Board proposed a tunnel three quarters of a mile below London Bridge.

This was considered by the Parliamentary committee in conjunction with a curious duplex bridge promoted by a private company, which was of course to be a toll bridge. In throwing out these proposals the committee suggested that an opening bridge should be provided in the neighbourhood of the Tower of London, and that the City Corporation with the funds of the Bridge House Estates should take up this crossing—which eventually became the Tower Bridge scheme, described in Chapter 12. The committee also authorized the Metropolitan Board of Works to go ahead with a steam ferry at Woolwich to compensate ratepayers in that area for their contribution toward toll abolition.

There were therefore two new free crossings of the river in

sight at the end of 1885; but there remained some nine miles of heavily built-up and industrialized tideway between these two points which were not served. Two sites for a tunnel came up for review, Shadwell and Blackwall, and the latter found favour as it would bring greater relief to a wider area. Sir Joseph Bazalgette therefore prepared plans and the Blackwall Tunnel Bill was passed in 1887 with practically no opposition.

The Blackwall Tunnel proposal was in fact the swansong of the Metropolitan Board of Works. Having obtained power to build the tunnel for a sum of £1,500,000 the Board was asked to leave the placing of the contract for the work to its successor, the London County Council. In spite of this the Board declared its intention of reaching a decision at its final meeting on 22nd March 1889. This so outraged the newly elected representatives of London that the Government was approached and an order was made dissolving the Board on 21st March. Thus it was the Blackwall Tunnel which brought the Board which had achieved so much to an undignified end.

The Board had invited tenders for separate tunnels for foot passengers and for vehicles. The LCC, however, took advice and by 1890 their engineer-in-chief, Sir Alexander Binnie, after consulting Sir Benjamin Baker and Henry Greathead, adopted a single tunnel of 27 feet external diameter. It was to be constructed under air pressure, which was not to exceed 35 pounds per square inch.

The tunnel with its approaches was just over a mile in length, nearly 3,700 feet of which had to be driven under compressed air. In a paper read after the work was completed, Binnie was reassuring on the effects of pressure:

> I am often asked what it feels like in compressed air; this I think must in all cases be a personal matter. But summing up the result of my many weekly visits to the tunnel during the past two years, I should say that I feel no difference from that when under the ordinary atmospheric pressure. There is a very slight feeling of exhilaration if the pressure is over 20 lb. per square inch, probably caused by the larger amount of oxygen absorbed by the lungs, every one appears to speak with a nasal intonation, you cannot whistle, and the skin acts more freely than at the same temperature under normal conditions.

I should here note that no one becomes ill from the effects of compressed air while under its pressure; the baneful effects, if experienced at all, usually show themselves on coming out of it. But I have arrived at the conclusion that among otherwise healthy persons, some can and some cannot withstand air pressure, and I have had the pleasure of conducting many persons over the works, from little girls of 13 up to gentlemen of over 70 years of age, who have not felt the least ill effects from compressed air.

A massive shield was used for this operation, which in its day was the largest subaqueous work in the world. Twice the river water threatened, but did not stop the work, and in 1896 two thousand guests of the contractor sat down to a luncheon given in the workings 'which for the occasion was nicely draped, suggesting a marquee rather than a tunnel'.

This tunnel between Greenwich and Poplar, which Bazalgette did not live to see, is the one nineteenth-century tunnel which still serves its original purpose, though now doubled in size. Before these works below London Bridge were promoted and carried out there were a number of significant additions to the crossings of the tideway above the bridge. The creative talents of Joseph Bazalgette and the improving zeal of the Metropolitan Board of Works were much in evidence.

Some years before the Board was constituted, a Government commission had been appointed to 'enquire into and consider the most effectual means of improving the Metropolis and of providing increased facilities of communication within the same'. The outcome of this was a recommendation in 1842 that a suspension bridge should be built between the existing Battersea and Vauxhall Bridges 'from a point near Chelsea Hospital, on the north side, to a point near the public house called the Red House, on the south side'.

Apart from the building of Westminster Bridge, this was the only occasion in which a bridge was built by the Government on the recommendation of Parliament. In 1846 the Commissioners of H. M. Woods and Forests were authorized to build the first Chelsea Bridge. They were no less realistic than private enterprise in getting the money back. The total cost of the bridge, which opened in 1858, was about £95,000 and the bridge was to be made free as soon as £80,000 had been recouped from tolls. In 1863 a further sum of £11,000 was spent on strengthening the bridge. In 1875 it was made free for foot passengers on Sundays and public holidays but by that time the possibility of its being freed by toll payments had become more remote than ever, for it was estimated that over £85,000 was due for principal and arrears of interest after two decades of toll-taking. The Metropolitan Board of Works acquired it in 1879 and opened it free of toll, paying to H.M. Paymaster General the sum of £75,000. The toll-houses remained until the bridge was closed in 1935, to be superseded by the present suspension bridge carrying four lanes of traffic and costing £300,000, opened by the Prime Minister of Canada in May 1937.

Since the building of Westminster Bridge there had been a number of proposals for a bridge by the Palace at Lambeth on the site of the old horse-ferry. In 1836 a company obtained preliminary sanction but nothing came of it. In 1861 a new company was incorporated and the Lambeth Bridge Act passed. Before he became involved in the Tower Subway, Peter William Barlow was retained here to design a suspension bridge, which cost about £50,000 and was opened in 1862. It was acquired by the Metropolitan Board of Works in 1877 for just under £36,000 and given a ceremonial opening as a toll-free bridge by the Prince of Wales, afterwards King Edward VII.

Perhaps because it cost relatively little it gave great trouble. In 1887 Sir Benjamin Baker, the famous engineer, was called in to advise, and criticized the structure, to which temporary amendments were made. By 1892 the Bridges Committee of the LCC was already expressing the opinion that both Lambeth and Vauxhall should be reconstructed, but preference was given to Vauxhall Bridge. By 1905 all vehicles crossing Lambeth Bridge were limited to a walking pace. In 1910 the bridge was entirely closed to vehicular traffic and a slightly crazy arrangement was made which was solemnly described in an LCC handbook (1914): 'It has even been found necessary to prevent people from congregating on the bridge. When it is anticipated that crowds will collect, the bridge is entirely closed, gates having been provided at each end for the purpose. Notices of the intention to close the bridge are posted up at each end, when possible, before such a step is taken.' It was not superseded until 1932, by the present handsome steel bridge.

The 1870s saw the last two bridges to be promoted by private enterprise. The beautiful Albert Bridge, which in the seventies of this century still graces the river, and the Wandsworth Bridge, which might be considered to have taught shareholders a lesson.

The Wandsworth Bridge Act sanctioning the work in 1864 provided for a capital of £80,000. The estimate having proved inadequate, the promoting company returned to Parliament in 1867 for authorization of an extension of capital of £50,000. The company's engineer was Rowland Mason Ordish (1824–86) a distinguished engineer who had designed the roof of St Pancras Station and the Albert Hall, had been employed for the re-erection of the Crystal Palace at Sydenham and in 1858 had patented a 'straight chain suspension' system for bridges. Naturally the design he submitted to the company was for a suspension bridge similar to the Albert Bridge lower down the river, with which he was also connected. The company, however, made a change of plan, abandoning the suspension designs in favour of a lattice girder bridge, and Ordish resigned.

The delays and indecisions of the company were such that about ten years were lost before work started. As soon as the bridge opened in 1873 the company was involved in a dispute with the local authorities about the maintenance of the north bank approaches which, during the course of litigation, fell into such decay that the bridge which had cost £150,000 was producing a ridiculously small return. In 1874 the tolls amounted to £432 and only just managed to climb up to the sum of £1,100 for the year before the Metropolitan Board of Works acquired the bridge for £53,000. The long-suffering shareholders counted their losses while the Prince of Wales drove across it ceremoniously to declare it free of tolls. It was rebuilt just before the Second World War in 1938.

The building of Albert Bridge from Cadogan Pier, Chelsea, to Albert Road, Battersea, which opened in 1873, was first promoted in Parliament by the Albert Bridge Company about ten years earlier. At that time the population of Battersea and the surrounding district was increasing rapidly and there was an outcry for a

better means of crossing than that afforded by Chelsea Bridge to
the east of Battersea Park and Battersea Bridge to the west, which
was then little more than an antique timber viaduct. There was
little opposition to the project except from the owners of Battersea
Bridge, who managed to enforce an extraordinary guarantee from
the new company to pay £3,000 a year, spend £7,000 on urgent
repairs to the old bridge and to maintain it afterwards. Eventually
the Albert Bridge Company were forced to purchase Battersea
Bridge. This and the plans of the Metropolitan Board of Works
for the embankment held up the venture and for a period R. M.
Ordish, who had been retained from the outset as engineer, had
to stand by while others put forward rival designs for quick construction. Ultimately, with the experience he had gained in his
design and construction of the bridge over the Moldau in Prague
in 1868, he created the suspension bridge which, though cherished
as a period piece, has given rise to some doubts. In 1884 after the
Metropolitan Board of Works had taken over, Bazalgette directed
a considerable overhaul of the structure, costing more than
£25,000. In the seventies of this century a proposal has been put
forward to install a prop beneath the central suspended section.

Containment by embankment, by dock systems and by bridging
did not change the basic potency of that 'strong brown god',
which T. S. Eliot so rightly described as 'waiting, watching and
waiting. . . .' Peter de Colechurch's medieval bridge had demanded
constant attention throughout the six centuries. So it was not
surprising that so many of the bridges laid across the river by
speculative builders so soon fell victim to the tide's potencies and
to traffic conditions, and went on the sick list. The latter half of
the nineteenth century and the beginning of this century was a
period of constant patching up and rebuilding. Labelye's Westminster Bridge was already in trouble when Old London Bridge
was removed. Nearly every well-known engineer of the period had
had a hand in the repair of the failing structure when in 1844 a
Parliamentary committee was appointed to explore the possibility
of complete replacement. This committee amazed everybody by
recommending continued patching up of the old structure. For
nearly a decade committees succeeded one another, making
recommendations for and against the building of a new bridge,

and the delay had the advantage that the general scheme for the Thames embankments had already been planned by the time the project for a new bridge went ahead. The designs were by Thomas Page, who collaborated with Sir Charles Barry (1795–1860), architect of the Houses of Parliament. The new Houses of Parliament were opened before the bridge was completed in 1862 and the embankments came into use a year or so afterwards. It was fortunate that this coincidence of effort integrated the new bridge so handsomely with its surroundings. It consists of seven low segmental arches supported on granite piers, and cost about £250,000, the money deriving from property belonging to the Westminster Bridge Commissioners and from Parliamentary grants. It became a Government-owned bridge, being administered by the Office of Works until it was taken over by the Metropolitan Board of Works in 1887.

Mylne's Blackfriars Bridge was the next to disappear, when the City Corporation commissioned the present bridge designed by Joseph Cubitt (1811–72), the civil engineer who had constructed the Great Northern and the London, Chatham and Dover Railways. It was opened in 1869 by Queen Victoria, who drove on to open Holborn Viaduct.

A long-standing cross-river problem tackled by Sir Joseph Bazalgette was that of old Putney Bridge, a wooden viaduct built in 1729 originally offering twenty-eight openings, many of them only 14 feet wide. During the latter years of its obstructive existence some of the central piers were removed and replaced by iron girders giving a central opening of 72 feet. Alongside the old bridge was an aqueduct belonging to Chelsea Waterworks. The whole antique contraption had become a menace to navigation and an impediment to road traffic when the Metropolitan Board of Works took over, abolished the toll and built a new bridge to Bazalgette's design, which was opened in 1884.

After some fifty years of life, during which it gave a good return to its shareholders, the first suspension bridge at Hammersmith was condemned in the 1870s. A new suspension bridge designed by Tierney Clarke and costing about £80,000 received a royal opening from the Duke of Clarence in 1887, 'and it speaks very little for the judgement of our municipal authorities,' wrote

H. P. Clunn, 'that they failed to realise that a much wider structure would later become quite imperative.' It still retains a decorative quality which suits the annual festive occasion of the Boat Race.

When old Battersea Bridge fell into decay in the 1870s, Sir Joseph Bazalgette prepared the design for the new bridge, which was carried out under the direction of his son Edward, and was opened in 1890, with the adornment of two tracks of tramlines, one adjoining each kerb of the footway.

The nineteenth century closed with two major operations affecting the crossing of the river, the building of a weir and half-tidal lock at Richmond and the construction of the Tower Bridge.

The first of these, a most controversial measure in its time, lies half a mile downstream from Richmond Bridge and was described by the late A. P. Herbert as 'a good advertisement for the judicious use of dams'. Some two hours after high water three great gates are lowered across the river to hold the level of the water upstream and maintain it at a navigable level. During this period all craft use the lock. Two hours before the next high tide the gates are lifted again so that the arches are open for about four hours on every tide and the river is navigable all the time. The Act for the construction of this lock was passed in 1892 and provided for a footbridge across the river at this point. It restored to Richmond, Twickenham and Teddington the qualities of the 'Sweete Themmes' destroyed by the embankment and bridge construction work which had altered the nature of the tidal flow during the nineteenth century.

It remains for the last years of Queen Victoria's reign to create another crossing on a grand scale epitomizing the Victorian age. This was the opening of the Tower Bridge in 1894.

12

The Tower Bridge

In the Tower Bridge London found a symbol, majestic, exuberant and practical. Its planning and building reflected not only contemporary taste but two other qualities of the age—self-interest and ingenuity. As we have seen, the coming of the Metropolitan Board of Works and Sir Joseph Bazalgette had made an active issue of the need for river crossings east of the city. A bridge below the Tower of London had been widely acknowledged to be both desirable and practicable for two or three decades before the actual plan for the Tower Bridge was accepted. The reason for the long delay was the rejection by private interests and sometimes by the Corporation of London itself of successive schemes. The wharfingers in particular were resolutely against any plan which seemed to threaten their possession of the waterfront. In more general terms there was a prolongation of that conflict between navigation and road traffic which had loomed for centuries.

The projected bridge had to serve both interests, the needs of ocean-going shipping and relief for the congestion of commercial and industrial road traffic. This was a challenge to ingenuity which was accepted readily enough by the engineers and designers of the nineteenth century. No crossing was ever subject to such diversity of ingenious notions. In 1876 the Corporation Bridge Committee set up to study the problem and make recommendations considered a collection of schemes, some bordering upon the bizarre, which were afterwards summarized by Charles Welch as follows:

> Low Level Bridge, designed by Mr. Frederic Barnett, having in the middle a kind of loop or dock, without water-gates, allowing small craft to pass always, the swing only to be opened for large vessels. Approaching from each shore about one third its entire length, the bridge meets the loop, and diverges to the right and left, the traffic passing over one side of the loop by means of one of the swing or swivel bridges, the other swing bridge being left open for a vessel to pass in or out of the loop (and vice versa). The loop is divided by a platform longitudinally with the river, on each end of which turns one of the swings working the two openings by the same movement. By this means Mr. Barnett affirmed that large ships with the highest masts could pass without stopping the vehicular and passenger traffic. The cost was estimated at about £400,000 for works and property.
>
> A Movable or Rolling Bridge, to carry vehicles and passengers, proposed by Mr. G. Barclay Bruce, jun. By this arrangement a certain portion of the waterway was always to be left open for vessels. The river was to be divided into seven spans by six piers, on each of which would be fixed rollers and machinery for driving them. The bridge was to be 300 feet by 100 feet. As this kind of bridge might be placed at any level above high water, Mr. Bruce considered that it solved the question of approaches. He calculated that it could leave the shore every six minutes and carry upwards of 100 vehicles and 1,400 foot passengers. The cost of construction was to be £134,381 and the working expenses capitalized £10,000.
>
> Another Bridge similar to London Bridge to be built 100 feet eastward of it, and connected with it at each end, and at intermediate intervals, proposed by Mr. Thomas Chatfeild Clarke. No estimate of cost was given.
>
> Low Level Bridge, designed by Mr. John P. Drake. This was to be carried on girders, with a swing middle to turn on a pivot. Bridge to be 50 feet wide. No estimate of cost was given.
>
> High Level Bridge, proposed by Mr. Sidengham Duer, with a pair of hydraulic hoists at each end; bridge to be 40 feet wide and 740 feet long, girders 80 feet above high water mark. The hoists to be carried out on the principle of the Anderton lifts. No expense would be required for property compensation, as in the case of most high level bridges. The cost was estimated at £136,500 and the working expenses at £1,872 per annum.
>
> High Level Bridge of three spans, submitted by Mr. T. Glaxton Fidler. The centre span was to be of 508 feet, and the other two spans 180 feet each. The headway was to be 70 feet above Trinity

high water. The south approach was to be by means of a spiral ascent.

River Railway Line or Steam Ford, which Mr. C. T. Guthrie proposed to construct at the bottom of the river, carrying above a framed staging and deck, projecting above the level of high water. The carriage would be driven by machinery and move on the submerged lines between two quays. The estimated cost was £30,000.

Subway Double Cast-iron Arch, or 'sub-riverian arcade' resting on concrete bed, proposed by Mr. John Keith. Roadway to be 55 feet wide. The cost was to be £509,536.

High Level Bridge, proposed by Mr. Edward Perrett, with hydraulic hoists, the bridge to consist of three spans of 267 feet each and 80 feet above high water in centre; staircases to be provided for foot-passengers. Estimated cost £340,000 with £4,000 per annum additional for working expenses.

Two Paddle-wheel Ferry Boats, suggested by Mr. E. Waller (Thames Steam Ferry Company), to ply across, each 82 feet by 27 feet between paddle-boxes. Each boat was to carry twelve two-horse vans and 250 foot-passengers. Estimated outlay £55,000 and £8,000 per annum for working expenses.

These curious devices were turned down but the flow of suggestions continued. There was the duplex bridge already mentioned, which was first put forward by F. J. Palmer in 1877 and later integrated into the proposal of a private company in 1884. It consisted of two locks, semi-circular in shape, with sliding spans to allow shipping to enter. A span would then be closed to allow traffic to move while the opposite span would slide away to allow the shipping to move on.

What was described as a high level tunnel was put forward by Messrs Maynard and Cooke. The roof of this was to be not much below the bed of the river, thus doing away with the need for either lifts or long and steep approaches. These ingenious partners proposed that the tunnel would be built on the shore in 60-foot lengths of wrought-iron plates and arched similar to a ship. It was to be lined with a brick and concrete casing affording a roadway 38 feet wide and two footways each 8½ feet wide. As each section was completed on the shore it was proposed to close its ends and float it out until it was vertically over its desired position. Then it was to be sunk to its final place as a caisson.

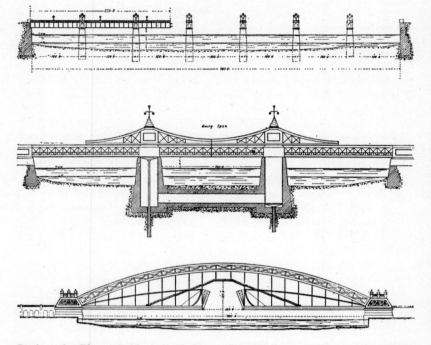

Designs for Tower Bridge: (top) George Barclay Bruce, 1876; (centre) Messrs Kinipple and Morris, 1884; (below) Messrs Ordish and Matheson, 1885.

Henry Vignoles put forward a scheme for a high level bridge structure with 85 feet clear headway in the centre at low water, with piers 300 feet apart spanned by parallel girders. To approach the platform of the bridge he envisaged spiral roads winding their way round huge blocks, to be 'utilized as might have been later found expedient'.

By 1883 the whole issue of a crossing at the Tower had become of such public interest that the London Chamber of Commerce held an exhibition of designs. There were eleven exhibits, including bridges, tunnels and the platform that travelled on rails.

With the wilder notions dismissed, two schemes, both the work of professionals, emerged. That by the City Architect, Horace Jones, was at first rejected but proved to be acceptable after a lapse of some ten years. The other, which nearly succeeded, was a magnificent medium level single-span bridge of 850 feet with a

Design for Tower Bridge by F. J. Palmer, 1877.

65-foot clearance above high water, designed by Bazalgette. The Metropolitan Board of Works applied to Parliament with this design in 1879. One of its practical disadvantages was difficulty of road access. There was to have been a long spiral ramp on the south bank to bring traffic up to the right level. The idea was opposed by the wharfingers, who claimed that the clearance for shipping was inadequate, and by the City Corporation, who already controlled Blackfriars and London Bridges and did not wish to see a new bridge built in their territory by the Metropolitan Board.

In the last chapter we referred to the Government decision made in 1884 to assign to the City Corporation through the Bridge House Estates the task of bridging the river while the Metropolitan Board went ahead with the Woolwich Free Ferry and the Blackwall Tunnel. So when the Corporation promoted the Tower Bridge Act in 1885 it was the bascule design of their own architect Horace Jones, originally submitted in 1878, which found favour. That John Wolfe Barry was appointed to join him as engineer was fortunate: for Jones, who was knighted after the Prince of Wales laid the foundation stone, died within a year of the work starting

and Barry—also knighted later—not only improved Jones's
designs while he was alive but was in a position to take over at his
death. It was the engineering skill and technical panache of Sir
John Wolfe Barry, appropriately partnered by Henry Marc
Brunel (the third generation of engineers) which realized the
singular and majestic character of Horace Jones's architectural
design. Barry wrote his own account of the affair modestly enough:

> When an opening bridge was first proposed there was some outcry
> by aesthetical people lest it should ruin the picturesqueness of
> the Tower of London by hideous girder erections, and it seemed
> to be the universal wish that this bridge should be in harmony
> architecturally with the Tower.
>
> To carry out these views various architectural studies were
> made, and it was originally intended by Sir Horace Jones, the
> City architect, that the towers be of brickwork in a feudal style of
> architecture, and that the bridge should be raised and lowered by
> chains somewhat like the drawbridge of a Crusader's castle. . . .
>
> The ideas were in this condition when the writer was appointed
> engineer to the scheme, with Sir Horace Jones as architect, and
> the Corporation went to Parliament for powers to make the bridge.
> It was seen that any arched form of construction across a span to
> be used by masted ships was inadmissible, and that whatever
> headway was given should be absolutely free of obstruction
> through the whole width of the span. Sir Horace Jones unfortun-
> ately died in 1887, when the foundations had not made much
> progress, and up to that time none of the architectural designs
> had proceeded further than such sketches and studies as were
> barely sufficient to enable an approximate estimate to be made of
> the cost. . . .
>
> The width, and consequently the weight, of the bridge was
> increased by the requirements of Parliament, and the span of the
> central opening was enlarged from 160 feet, as originally intended,
> to 200 feet. At the same time the provision of lifts and stairs to
> accommodate foot passengers when the bridge was open was felt
> to be a necessity.
>
> In this way it became apparent that it would not be possible to
> support the weight of the bridge on towers wholly of masonry, as
> in the first designs, unless they were made of great size and un-
> necessary weight. It was consequently requisite that the main
> supports should be of iron or steel, which could, however, be
> surrounded by masonry, so as to retain the architectural character
> of the whole structure.
>
> It was clear that in any event a large part of the steelwork of the

towers must be enclosed in some material, for the moving quadrants project upwards some 40 feet from the level of the roadway, while the stairs and lifts also required protection from the weather. It thus became a question of surrounding the towers either with cast-iron panelling or with stone, and eventually a granite facing, with Portland stone dressings, was adopted.

Aesthetically speaking, stone seems better than cast-iron, which would equally hide the constructive features, and practically speaking it is also better, when it is considered that there is no mode so satisfactory for preserving iron or steel from corrosion as embedding it in brickwork, concrete or masonry.

Barry went on to describe the towers as being 'steel skeletons clothed with stone', and then added: 'It is to be feared some purists will say that the lamp of truth has been sadly neglected in this combination of materials, and that the architects of classical or mediaeval times would not have sanctioned such an arrangement as a complex structure of steel surrounded by stone.'

One reason may be that the architects of those ages did not know much about iron or steel. Perhaps if they had been acquainted with their capabilities they might have been as ready to employ them as they were to back up stone-faced walls with brick, as Sir Christopher Wren did when he used a brick cone to support the internal and external domes of St Paul's.

However all this may be, 'needs must when Parliament drives', and if the appearance of the Tower Bridge is approved, we may forget that the towers have skeletons as much concealed as that of the human body, of which we do not think when we contemplate examples of manly or feminine beauty.

The building of the bridge took eight years and cost £902,500 exclusive of the approaches. Not least of the difficulties in construction was that 160 feet of the central fairway of the river had always to be kept open, making it impossible to build more than one pier foundation at a time. This condition had been laid down by the Thames Conservancy representing navigational interests when the bridge Bill went through Parliament, and it was the same influence which dictated a condition that the finished bridge was to remain open for two hours at each high tide. This triumph of the nautical interests over those of road users was the reason for the building of the raised footway between the towers 142 feet above high water level for the use of pedestrians while the bascules were raised. This footway, with access by stairs and lifts, was eventually closed to the public in 1911.

In the construction and operation of the bridge there are several unique curiosities. Owing to its proximity to the Tower and the need for a small encroachment on the Tower Ditch in making the approaches, the military authorities of the day were able to make some conditions of their own. They required that the architecture of the bridge should be in harmony with that of the Tower, and they appear to have been easily satisfied on that score. At first they seemed to imply that they wished the bridge to be fortified but did not press this. They settled for free access and the right to occupy the bridge at any time.

To meet the contingency of sailing vessels being becalmed and unable to make the passage through the bridge a tug is permanently stationed on the north-west side, ready for instant action. The continued presence of this is often misconstrued as a stand-by for the rescue of potential suicides.

Stables were built into the bridge and until the 1930s trace-horses were kept to assist horse-drawn vehicles across the bridge, and alleviate the congestion caused so frequently in former times by fallen horses.

The priorities at Tower Bridge were always clear. Shipping came first—and it still does. It is a proud tradition that the bridge has never failed to lift for a ship. By day or by night any vessel, having a mast or superstructure 30 feet high or more, approaching from the east upon passing Cherry Garden Pier, Rotherhithe, may transmit a signal to the Bridge requiring it to be opened. Any similar vessel casting off from the Pool of London may request the opening of the bridge. The opening takes from seven to ten minutes from receipt of the signal. There is no question at any time of river traffic being kept waiting. It is road traffic which awaits the convenience of navigation.

Because of its navigational duties the Tower Bridge is unique among London bridges in carrying a substantial staff of men on twenty-four-hour watch. Eighty men are employed in all with fourteen on watch at any one time. They are under the command of the Superintendent Engineer and Bridgemaster who, when he is not on duty in his office on one of the abutments, occupies an official residence on the southern approach.

When the bridge is to be raised the watch on duty alert the police stationed on the spot and the cross bridge traffic is stopped by lights. The system has not always proved infallible in the past. On one occasion the driver of a double-decker bus overshot the lights and jumped his vehicle across the gap just as the bridge was opening.

Great steam engines beneath the southern approaches power the bridge machinery. As examples of Victorian steam engineering they are outstanding and should be regarded as one of the sights of London, whatever the future may hold for them. At the time of writing the use of the bridge is rapidly diminishing. The report of the Planning and Communications Committee of the City Corporation of September 1970 stated: 'During the past twelve months a more rapid change has occurred in the movement of shipping using the Upper Pool, i.e. that part of the River Thames between Tower Bridge and London Bridge, than could have been anticipated. This is due to the closure of all wharves in the Upper Pool. This means that there are now no ocean-going ships using the Upper Pool on a regular basis.

'It would appear, therefore, that only occasional users can be expected for the foreseeable future, such as ships forming part of a State occasion or visits by the Royal Navy or Foreign Navies; Training Ships, Yachts, &c. . . .'

The report went on to suggest either the permanent closure of the bridge, thereby restricting the river westwards to river traffic only: or modernization of the machinery, so that 'it remains capable of being maintained and opened on an economic basis'.

It is not so much that priorities have changed as that conditions have changed in that there are fewer ships and no large ones. What goes over Tower Bridge is now more significant than that which passes beneath. The bridge is inadequate for the traffic of the 1970s though it is structurally sound. Its complex machinery built to serve the needs of navigation is almost redundant. Its future may well be more decorative than practical. Fortunately there is no question of its being condemned out of hand as an obsolete structure and swept away ruthlessly, like old London

Bridge. It has achieved a unique situation as a symbol of London and as perhaps the most visited and nationally cherished of the world's bridges.

During the Second World War, when it carried an anti-aircraft battery, the bridge was singled out for much more attention than this small fortification deserved. Referring to the Nazi flying bombs Sir Winston Churchill stated: 'All were aimed at Tower Bridge. . . .' but they fell 'far and wide over the country-side from Hampshire to Suffolk.' On a sunny morning in July 1944 one of the so-called 'doodlebugs' came through the central arch of the bridge and landed on the Tower Bridge tug. At that moment one crew was relieving the other and both were lost. There were two or three more near misses but though Charing Cross bridge was disabled the Tower Bridge remained unscathed by these weapons.

After surviving the war it is particularly fortunate that the bridge is not too greatly threatened by financial pressures. Its maintenance is not a burden upon London's rates or the nation's taxes. It is looked after from funds provided by the Bridge House Estates, a beneficiary of the pious offerings of medieval Londoners.

13

East of the Tower

Except for railway construction, private speculation took no further part in the crossings of the Thames in the twentieth century: all the work has been planned and carried out by public authorities.

The bridge pattern of the nineteenth century has only had two additions, both in the western suburbs—at Chiswick and Twickenham. Seven of the established bridges have been rebuilt. Otherwise the additional crossings have been by tunnel—for pedestrians and wheeled traffic to the east of London Bridge and for railways in the central area.

With the Tower Bridge completed and the Blackwall Tunnel opened at the turn of the century, the LCC Bridges Committee was still under pressure to provide further free crossings between these points. 'It was pointed out,' wrote G. L. Gomme, the Clerk of the Council, 'that if Deptford Broadway was taken on the south and Millwall Dock Station on the north, a distance of about $1\frac{1}{2}$ miles in a straight line, a person who wished to get from one to the other, would, by using the existing means of communication, have to traverse a distance of about $7\frac{1}{2}$ miles if he went by the Tower Bridge, or $9\frac{1}{2}$ miles if he used the Woolwich Ferry. The distance would be reduced on the opening of the Blackwall Tunnel, but even then it would not be less than $4\frac{1}{2}$ miles. Direct means of communication between Greenwich and Millwall would, however, reduce the distance to $2\frac{1}{2}$ miles.'

The Council was cautious about the construction of another big vehicular tunnel until Blackwall had proved itself. Though the Free Ferry at Woolwich was running successfully the Thames Conservancy was against the establishment of further ferries on the grounds that they were an impediment to river traffic.

A ferry attempt which had failed had been made by the Thames Steam Ferry Company in 1887. They had deliberately selected a site directly over Brunel's tunnel, because no vessels were allowed to moor within a certain distance of the line of the tunnel and the ferry boats could have a clear passage in that crowded part of the river. The ferry boats were designed to convey twelve two-horse wagons each way, in addition to foot passengers, every fifteen minutes. To cope with the rise and fall of the tide hydraulic lifts were installed. These were 80 feet long and 45 feet wide, capable of a load of fifty tons. On one occasion there were eight two-horse drays and one or two smaller vehicles on the lift. In June 1881 over 7,000 horses and 5,000 vehicles used the ferry, the working expenses of which averaged about £100 a week. In a subsequent inquiry into the running of the ferry a carman gave evidence that 'he with a team of three horses had frequently used the lifts and that the animals took no notice of being raised and lowered and were as quiet as when in their stables'.

This ferry failed to make a profit and was withdrawn after a few years. The difficulty with all ferries, more particularly in Victorian times when river traffic was so heavy, was fog and ice.

At the last meeting of the London and Tilbury Lighterage Company [wrote J. E. Tuit in 1893], it was stated that during the year there were twenty-seven days on which work was more or less suspended on the river owing to fog; and during the three years 1879 to 1881 there were on the average thirty-eight days on which fogs were so dense that the South-Eastern Railway Company could not work its trains between Cannon-street and Charing Cross without using fog signals and experiencing delays. To this should be added twelve days of frost, making fifty days in the year on which ferries would be unable to work. For the last two winters, during the construction of the Tower Bridge, it has been impossible to row across the river for weeks together, on account of accumulations of floating ice.

At Greenwich the ferry hazards were particularly bad, and the

Clerk to the LCC wrote: 'It was pointed out that such was the feeling of uncertainty engendered in the case of the existing ferry at Greenwich that some of the employers on the Isle of Dogs would not allow their principal men to live on the Greenwich side of the river, but insisted on their living on the island, as it was essential for the purposes of their business that foremen and first-class mechanics should not be late.'

So the Council committed itself to the building of the subway between Greenwich and the Isle of Dogs at an estimated cost of just over £70,000, which did not include compensation, and the Thames Tunnel (Greenwich to Millwall) Act was duly passed. The question of compensation rested upon this clause in the Bill.

> The Licensed Ferrymen of the Company of Watermen and Lightermen of the River Thames who now are and have been working from Upper Watergate, Deptford, to Cocoa Nut Stairs, Millwall, for three years before the passing of this Act (including any person who was an apprentice to any such Ferryman at any time within the said period of three years, and shall be a Licensed Ferryman working between the said points at the time of the opening of the subway) shall be entitled after the opening of the subway to such sum by way of compensation as may be determined to be fair and reasonable by an arbitrator to be appointed by the Board of Trade.

While the Bill was still in committee the watermen came forward with the suggestion that arbitration would be a costly method for both sides of settling their claims. They asked that £150 should be paid to each of the licensed ferrymen by way of immediate compensation. The Council settled for a payment of £100 to be made to each man 'on the commencement of the subway, the agreement being limited to the men (24 in number) named in it'. Thus the subway proposal terminated the affairs of one of the oldest ferries of the tideway. In 1550 Edward VI granted the lordships and manors of Stepney and Hackney to Sir Thomas Wentworth and these included with their rights that of running the ferry, which was first described as Potter's Ferry. A more specific reference to the ferry was in 1654 when The Commissioners for the Estates of Delinquents sold it to William Smith and Joseph Drew. Samuel Pepys used the ferry twice in the year

1665 and it was evidently an important link in the line of communication between Greenwich and the centre of London.

The Warner family purchased the ferry in 1676, and in 1762 Richard Warner granted to certain watermen of Greenwich:

> all that his ferry place, then commonly called or known by the name of Potter's Ferry, with the ferryage, waftage, and passage for men, horses, beasts, and all other cattle and carriages whatsoever, over the river Thames, lying, being, and extending itself from a place or marsh called the Isle of Dogs or Stebunheath Marsh, over the said river unto the town of Greenwich, in the county of Kent.

While the ferry was owned by the Warners there was a dispute between the Greenwich Watermen and the Watermen's Company because the men 'do work on the Lord's Day across the river, from Greenwich to the Isle of Dogs, and exact large prices for passengers to pass and repass across the river there'. The company resolved 'that no more pensioners be admitted from the town of Greenwich, by reason of the watermen of that town laying claim to the Sunday ferry there'.

In 1794 certain watermen held the ferry in trust for the Potter's Ferry Society. In 1812 a horse ferry was established by Act of Parliament creating a statutory ferry for horses and vehicles in favour of the Poplar and Greenwich Ferry Company, which was empowered to construct and take tolls for certain roads on the Isle of Dogs approaching the ferry. The Potter's Ferry Society meanwhile retained its right to carry foot passengers.

In 1883 the Metropolitan Board of Works bought out the company, extinguished the ferry and freed the Isle of Dogs roads from toll. The Potter's Ferry continued to operate for foot passengers only. The Society leased it first to the Thames Steamboat Company, from whom it was afterwards conveyed to the London and Blackwall Railway Company, which ultimately became part of the Great Eastern Railway Company system. Though its operation was much criticized, its traffic was considerable. 'Notwithstanding the grave objections and hindrances to a steamboat-ferry in a crowded river like the Thames,' wrote William Charles Copperthwaite, who became resident engineer at the new subway, 'the yearly traffic amounts to about 1,300,000 passengers.'

The railway was of course one of the interests which had to be compensated. At first the Council contended that the cross-river subway would bring so much new business to the railway that no compensation was called for. Eventually, however, the railway received £8,000 for the ferry rights. In addition to this a short subway was built connecting the North Greenwich station with the river crossing. The railway ceased to carry passengers in 1926, and the station has now vanished from the scene.

Even at the beginning of the nineteenth century the vagaries of the ferry service between Greenwich and the Isle of Dogs had been under criticism. As early as 1812, soon after Trevithick's efforts had failed, a proposal had been made to build a tunnel almost on the site of the Greenwich subway but the scheme had failed. The first Parliamentary Bill, The Greenwich and Millwall Subway Act, was passed in 1877. Though its powers were extended several times nothing was done until the London County Council obtained its Act in 1899. Work began in June that year and the subway was opened to the public without ceremony on August Bank Holiday 1902.

Sir Alexander Binnie, who had worked on the Blackwall Tunnel, designed the subway, which is just over 1,200 feet long. At each end pedestrian access is by stairway and by the lifts which were installed a year or so after the opening. The Poplar shaft is 44 feet deep; the shaft at Greenwich where the entrance faces the *Cutty Sark* is 50 feet deep. The bill was a few pounds short of £180,000 of which some £58,000 went on acquisition of property and payment of compensation. In 1903, the first full year of operation, just under 4,000,000 foot passengers used the tunnel.

Over 4,000,000 foot passengers and 335,000 vehicles had used Blackwall Tunnel in its first full year of operation and the figure for vehicles had already more than doubled by the time the Greenwich Tunnel had been finished. The London County Council therefore felt that it was well justified in going ahead with the Rotherhithe Tunnel between Lower Road, Rotherhithe and Commercial Road East, Stepney.

Since the first planning proposals put forward by Sir Joseph Bazalgette it had been considered by everyone concerned that a crossing was needed at this point so near to that achieved by the

Brunels with their tunnel and for a short time by the Thames
Steam Ferry Company. After starting on Tower Bridge the LCC
applied in 1892 for powers to establish a steamboat ferry at
Rotherhithe. The Thames Conservancy opposed this as an
impediment to navigation and it had to be dropped. It was not
until 1900 that the Council managed to obtain the Thames Tunnel
(Rotherhithe and Ratcliff) Act, after meeting considerable
opposition in the Lords and the Commons. Work on the tunnel
began in 1904, the chief engineer being Mr, later Sir, Maurice
Fitzmaurice.

Compared with the agonies suffered on that site by the Brunels
and their workpeople, the construction work was swift and
efficient. The contract time allowed was five and a half years yet
the job was finished in a little over four years. There were no
casualties among the 800 men engaged in the work, though 450
of them were working in compressed air. The undertaking, however, was not without its hazards. In describing the tunnel, the
overall length of which is one and a quarter miles, G. L. Gomme
wrote:

> the under-river portion, about 1,500 feet long between the shafts,
> crosses under the River Thames in a diagonal direction. In
> addition to that portion of the tunnel actually under the river,
> very great difficulties with water were encountered in the approach
> tunnels for very long lengths on each side. In the centre of the
> Thames the tunnel is only about 7 feet below the bed of the river.
> In the case of the Blackwall Tunnel the Thames Conservancy
> allowed about 10 feet of clay to be placed on the river bed while
> the tunnel was under construction, so as to give more cover over-
> head. In the present case, owing to the work being constructed
> opposite both the Surrey Commercial Docks and the London
> Docks, the Thames Conservancy were unable to give permission
> for any clay to be placed on the bed of the river. The work, there-
> fore, had to be carried out with the greatest possible care, and
> every precaution possible was taken to ensure the safety of the men
> in the tunnel in the event of the 7 feet of sand between the top of
> the tunnel and the bed of the river giving way during construc-
> tion, and so carefully was the work carried out that at no time did
> the river break in.

The tunnel was opened by the Prince of Wales, afterwards King

George V, in June 1908. The ferrymen were compensated for loss of earnings. An arbitration awarded £1,835 to 58 watermen of a total of 135 who put in claims. In the first full year after its opening nearly 2,400,000 passengers and 950,000 vehicles used the tunnel.

Before coming to the fourth of the tunnels built by the LCC and opened at Woolwich in 1912, we must revert to that district where we left it in the last century in Chapter 5 (see p. 5).

The Woolwich Ferry, opened in 1889, was the first achievement of the old Metropolitan Board of Works in providing free crossing of the river east of London Bridge. The total cost was just on £192,000, including the first three ferry boats the *Duncan*, the *Hutton* and the *Gordon* (named after the hero of Khartoum, who was born in Woolwich). This figure included compensation for loss of income paid to the 'Watermen and Lightermen of Woolwich', though some of these at least continued to ply their oars; to the Woolwich (Old Barge House) Steam Ferry Company, which went into liquidation; and to the Great Eastern Railway Company, which received £27,500 though it continued to run its Penny Ferry in competition with the Free Ferry until 1908. When it finally gave up, the *Kentish Independent*'s obituary declared: 'For just over 60 years captains and crews have carried on manfully, spring, summer, autumn and winter, bravely facing the dangers of cross-river navigation, ever so cheery as the cricket that chirps on the kitchen hearth.'

The Free Ferry opened with 'quite extraordinary public rejoicing' and became imbued, more than any other river-crossing since Old London Bridge, with a social as well as a utilitarian life. Generations of Woolwich mothers took their families on board the old paddle boats to picnic and spend the afternoon on the water free-riding between Essex and Kent shores.

> . . . these, the original steamers [wrote E. F. E. Jefferson in *The Woolwich Story*] were the children's playtime paradise. Apart from the mere joy of being afloat, with the clang of bells, splash of paddle-wheel creating artificial soap suds, gleam and glow and heat and oil-smell in the engine room, foam, wind and spray on deck, there were steps to climb, capstan and anchor, chain and rope to chase around, a nice long run from bow to stern and,

best of all, a warm iron casing where the water boiled, so shaped as to provide a lovely slide some six foot from top to bottom. Then there was the possibility that a member of the crew would suddenly pop up from the secret, dark lower regions to put a stop to all pranks. He would turn you off, too, when the boat tied up; but he could not stop you running all the way up the steps, along and down the other side of the pontoon, to re-embark and sit quiet until the ropes were cast off, the paddles throbbed and the vessel got under way again.

The original three boats were followed by four more paddle steamers built in the 1920s, one of which was named the *Squires* after a prominent Woolwich bookseller. The boilers of these vessels did not offer the same sliding facilities for the young though they were popular socially and between them would carry 20,000 passengers and 2,300 vehicles in one day. One of the old ferry captains on his retirement in the 1920s declared: 'Even in clear weather you want your wits about you and about forty pairs of eyes. It's like an old lady getting from one side to the other of a busy highway in the heart of London with no policeman to help her.'

There was only one serious mishap during the period. On a June evening in 1926 the *Squires* arrived alongside the south pontoon with 400 passengers on board, and her ropes had just been made fast when the mate, Reuben Edmonds, who was in charge saw an American steamer of 6,000 tons, *Coahoma County*, steering a peculiar course and heading downriver toward the ferry boat. Reuben instantly gave orders for the ropes to be cast off and for the engines to go full speed astern. This swift action saved the *Squires* from being sunk at her moorings but she still suffered a crushing blow on her port bow, which caused her to rebound onto the pier. Most of her passengers, who had been standing ready to disembark, were thrown about as the ferry drifted out into midstream, one engine out of action, her rails gone. No one was killed but eleven injured went to hospital.

Since its inauguration to the present day when the paddle steamers have given way to diesel-engined boats the Free Ferry has only been closed three times—following the *Squires* accident, during the General Strike in 1926 and in 1949 for pontoon repair. During the Second World War it maintained a twenty-four hour service as and when needed, having no guide lights whatever in the blackout. During the most ferocious raid on the docks on 7th September 1940 the ferries plied to and fro all night across the tideway, scattered with burning oil, evacuating the people of Silvertown with their belongings from the blazing Essex shore.

Throughout the years, however, fog and sometimes ice militated against the continuous working of the ferry. With the increased growth of population and industry at the turn of the century the stoppages recorded were particularly serious, for they usually occurred during the early mornings when so many made the crossing to work. During 1900–7 the ferry was suspended owing to fog for an average of 104 hours a year. The building of a tunnel to supplement the ferry services was the obvious answer.

Even in 1874, some time before the arrival of the Free Ferry, an Act of Parliament had been obtained by a private company to build such a tunnel. Preparations had been made for the use of a shield and air-locks when the scheme was abandoned in 1876. While the LCC was still undecided on the issue, another private company went to Parliament with the North and South Woolwich Railway Bill in 1904. This was for the construction of a tunnel to carry a shuttle service of electric trains, and it attracted much popular support though it entailed paying to cross the river. The LCC did not directly oppose it but simply pointed out the large sums of public money paid out in compensation for the Free Ferry and proposed that the Bill should not be allowed unless the company agreed not to oppose the building of a free tunnel or to seek compensation if one was built.

This killed the Bill though it was some years before the LCC, owing to such commitments as the rebuilding of Vauxhall Bridge and the making of Rotherhithe Tunnel, was ready to go ahead. Sir Maurice Fitzmaurice was in charge of the construction, which closely resembled that of the Greenwich tunnel—a cast-iron tube pedestrian subway served by stairs and lifts at either end— and it was opened in 1912.

As soon as it was in use the Council was able to cut down on what had become almost a continuous service of ferry boats, for the tunnel and the ferry were regarded as complementary. The fleet of three ferry boats which came into service in the 1920s, each burning roughly eight tons of coke a day, ran until the 1960s, when they were superseded by three diesel vessels named after pioneering politicians, the *John Burns*, the *James Newman* and the *Ernest Bevin* (who was 'the dockers' KC' and represented Woolwich in Parliament). The old paddle steamers had been adequate for the horse-drawn vehicles and lighter traffic of the past, being designed for side loading. Heavier and articulated types of vehicles had become increasingly difficult to stow. So the new boats were end-loading, and to serve them terminals were built with mechanically operated hinged traffic bridges to make loading and off-loading easier. The ferry boats which are double ended are each capable of transporting a thousand passengers and two hundred tons of vehicles. By the 1970s they were carrying in an average week in May 28,152 vehicles, making 1,033 trips to do this.

14

The Twentieth Century

While engaged upon the building of the Tower Bridge Sir John Wolfe Barry was called in to examine the structure of Tunstall's Kew Bridge, which had been opened in 1789 and was therefore just over one hundred years old and considered to be in urgent need of widening and improvement. The foundations of the piers were found to be unsatisfactory and Barry also reported that there was no practical way of improving the steep gradients. So an Act of Parliament was obtained in 1898 for the construction of a new bridge, a joint enterprise of the county councils of Surrey and Middlesex. A temporary wooden bridge was erected in 1899 before Tunstall's stone bridge was demolished. The new bridge consisting of three elliptical arches was opened by King Edward VII in 1903.

Vauxhall Bridge, which had been opened the year after the Battle of Waterloo and acquired by the old Metropolitan Board of Works in 1879, was the next casualty. In the 1880s two of the central piers of the bridge had been removed because they had been an impediment to river traffic. Soon after this work was done it was found that the scour of the river was damaging the foundations of the bridge and powers to rebuild it were obtained. The actual rebuilding dragged on from 1898 to 1906 when the bridge, decorated by bronze statues of heroic size designed by Messrs Pomeroy and Drury, both of the Royal Academy, was opened to the public. It was the first bridge in London to be crossed by tramcars. The cost, which came to about £2,000,000, for a time had held up the Council's development of the Woolwich tunnel.

Meanwhile the Thames was being crossed again by the first of a series of tunnels carrying the London tube system. 'Today London's newest blue-clay thoroughfare will be thrown open to the huge traffic which will undoubtedly make use of it,' announced *The Sphere* of 10th March 1906.

> The new line stretches from Kensington through Waterloo to Baker Street. The name, Waterloo and Baker Street, is somewhat a misnomer as since the line was originally planned powers to extend both ends have been obtained, the south end to the Elephant and Castle and the north end to Paddington. The section which opens today includes the Kennington Road Station and Baker Street.

The consultant on this penetration of the tube railway system beneath the river was Sir Benjamin Baker, already mentioned in connection with the City and South London, who had received his knighthood at the opening of the Forth Bridge, which he had designed. His most curious undertaking had been his design for a wrought-iron caisson for the towing of Cleopatra's Needle from Egypt to London. In addition to the Bakerloo, he was responsible for the tunnelling of the Central London railway. Subsequently the London underground railway system had five separate tunnels beneath the Thames.

At a meeting of the Institution of Civil Engineers, after papers had been read describing the Bakerloo subaqueous tunnel and the Greenwich pedestrian subway, it was suggested by Sir Maurice Fitzmaurice that engineers in this century could contemplate tunnelling beneath the river 'with the same confidence as they would start building a house'. The railway tunnelling beneath the Thames proceeded as undramatically as he suggested.

From the completion of Vauxhall Bridge in 1906 until after the First World War no new crossings of the Thames were made nor were any of the old bridges reconstructed. A bridge at St Paul's was proposed in 1911 and a great deal of property was acquired for the approaches, but after a number of extensions of time for the work the House of Commons in 1929 finally refused to make any further extensions and the project was abandoned.

After the First World War Rennie's Southwark Bridge was removed and the Corporation of London built a new bridge to the design of Sir Ernest George, which was opened by King George V in 1921.

Peter Barlow's old iron suspension bridge at Lambeth mentioned in Chapter 11 (see p. 124), which had been virtually out of use for years, was demolished in 1929, and in 1932 King George V opened a new bridge carrying four lanes of traffic and costing some £440,000. It was designed by Sir George Humphreys in collaboration with Sir Reginald Blomfield.

The following year saw something of a record in the opening of three brand new Thames bridges, all of them joint County Council enterprises and all of them opened by the then Prince of Wales (later King Edward VIII) on 3rd July 1933. One of these at Hampton Court lies above the tideway and outside the scope of these pages. The other two, Chiswick Bridge, designed by Sir Herbert Baker and having the longest concrete arch of any bridge on the Thames, linking Chiswick and Mortlake, and Twickenham Bridge, by Maxwell Ayrton, linking Richmond with Twickenham, were significant in that they fulfilled an arterial pattern of transport opening up the approaches to the west and south west of the metropolis. They represented a twentieth-century conception in that they served not so much local residential and commercial needs as the more strategic purposes of through traffic.

Large-scale traffic movements providing a link for the south circular road with the road network north of the Thames were an important element in the decision by the LCC to rebuild Wandsworth Bridge, replacing the 1873 bridge which had a carriageway only 18 feet wide with a bridge to take four lanes of traffic. This was opened in 1938. Meanwhile in 1935 the old Chelsea suspension bridge built by the Commissioners of Woods and Forests was pulled down and replaced by a new suspension bridge carrying four lines of traffic, which was opened by the then Prime Minister of Canada, W. L. Mackenzie King. The bridge, which cost some £365,000, was designed by the engineers Messrs

Endel, Palmer and Tritton in collaboration with the Council's architect, with the Royal Fine Art Commission also in consultation.

While the reconstruction of river crossings to the west of London went forward in the period between the wars and the problems of the crossings to the east of London Bridge had been to some extent solved, a controversy built up over the vital central area of the metropolis—between Westminster and Blackfriars. From 1914 to 1937 the number of vehicles crossing the river in London had doubled, and a large share of this pressure fell upon Rennie's Waterloo Bridge. It developed a dip at the Strand end and in 1923 it was found that it was not standing up to the traffic. It became necessary to shore up two of the arches. Two years later to relieve the pressure a temporary bridge had to be erected beside it. To prevent causing navigational obstruction this temporary bridge had a central span stretching the width of two of Rennie's arches and this pre-fabricated span was launched from the old bridge.

> The unusual, although perhaps not wholly unprecedented course [wrote *The Engineer*] was followed of erecting the 280 ft. navigation span on the roadway of the old bridge and of launching it sideways downstream into position across the gap. This procedure involved moving the span laterally through a distance of 93 ft. and of lowering it through about 12 ft. on to its piers. It might be thought that to erect a steel structure weighing some 500 tons on the roadway of a bridge that was patently giving way, was a risky proceeding. Actually, however, the stoppage of vehicular traffic across the bridge before the erection of the navigation span was begun relieved the old structure of a load not far different from that thrown upon it by the weight of the span. Moreover the removal of the parapets and other portions of the stone bridge to permit the span to be launched at a lower level than would otherwise have been imposed, reduced the weight on the old piers in keeping with the rate at which additional load was applied by the erection of the span.

The journal also offered a cool professional assessment of the controversial issue which was arising as the temporary bridge went up.

There are undoubtedly strong artistic and sentimental reasons why Rennie's bridge, which is acknowledged by all to be the most beautiful structure across the London river, should not be destroyed, and a large body of engineers and architects still hold fast to the opinion that it can be preserved. On the other hand, there are those who assert that the works of preservation are impracticable and that, even if the bridge could be restored to its old strength, it should be pulled down in order to make room for one of larger dimensions. As to widening the present bridge whilst preserving its present structure, it seems to be generally agreed that that course cannot be considered. The bridge is situated at a sharp bend in the river, and vessels up to 2,000 tons deadweight capacity carrying coal to the Wandsworth Gasworks have to pass it. Were the bridge much wider than it is at present, Rennie's arches would assume the form of narrow tunnels, which, in conjuction with the bend in the river, would form an inconvenient obstacle, if not an actual danger, to ships and barges passing up and down.

In the past individuals had expressed opinions about the aesthetic merits and shortcomings of London's bridges but there had been no organized bodies of public opinion, for instance to deplore the ruthless destruction of the fabric of old London Bridge or the railway companies slinging their utilitarian spans across the river. But now as the temporary bridge went up there was a 'conference of societies urging the preservation of Waterloo Bridge' and a huge pro-Rennie conservation lobby made itself heard aesthetically and felt politically. In 1926 a Royal Commission studied the subject of cross-river traffic in the London area. They recommended a scheme, which was widely condemned, for corbelling out the sides of the bridge to broaden the roadway, thus maintaining the Rennie outline. They linked this with recommendations for a new bridge and approaches at Charing Cross. Thus the destinies of Waterloo and Charing Cross bridges were for some years entangled. The Royal Commission referred to Charing Cross Bridge as 'an eyesore and a blot on one of the finest vistas in Europe'. In the course of the arguments which followed, a former chairman of the LCC, Captain George Swinton, cried: 'The bridge so many love is coming down, the bridge so many loathe still stands triumphant in its ugliness.'

The LCC had put forward a scheme for a new road bridge at Charing Cross in 1929 but the House of Commons rejected it then and again in 1931. The expense put it out of the range of possibility and it was shelved while the battle of Waterloo Bridge intensified, becoming more political than aesthetic. That renowned Labour politician, Herbert Morrison, had become Leader of the LCC, and champion for the cause of a new bridge at Waterloo. In his autobiography he afterwards wrote of '. . . Rennie's masterpiece. The bridge, too weak for heavy traffic, its blocked arches interfering with river navigation was, by some, regarded as an ancient monument. . . .' He went on that 'we argued that all great architects were not necessarily dead, and that in any case Rennie had been an engineer. In the heart of the capital we needed a traffic artery, not an ancient monument.' In *The Times* there were letters about 'the vulgar, utilitarian ideas of Mr Morrison'. Stanley Baldwin, the Tory Prime Minister, pronounced himself firmly on the side of the monument.

The cross-river conflict between the LCC on the south bank and Parliament at Westminster ran through most of the thirties. In 1932 the Council sought leave to spend money from capital on the demolition of the Rennie fabric and replacing it with a new bridge. The vigorous opposition to this succeeded and the provision relating to Waterloo Bridge was struck out of the Council's money bill. The following year the Council reluctantly decided to undertake the much-criticized scheme for reconditioning the bridge. In 1934, however, with a change of party, the Council rescinded this resolution and Parliament was approached once again, and after much heated debate turned down the provision relating to the new bridge. At that point Morrison and the LCC decided that a special penny rate for five years would pay for the bridge and that they would go ahead without any grant from Parliament. Morrison scandalized conservationists by loosening the first stone. 'Waterloo Bridge became a symbol of the new spirit at County Hall. G. R. Strauss, chairman of the Highways Committee, Reginald Pott, the vice-chairman and I had an unofficial ceremony at the bridge; between us we began the physical work of the demolition of the old bridge. We were warned by officers that the ceremony was unauthorized and irregular. We admitted that but we just could not resist removing a loose stone or two.'

The Council approached Parliament again in 1935 and was repulsed. Finally in 1937 the Minister of Transport announced that a grant of 60 per cent would be given by the Government for the cost of building a new bridge but not for demolishing the old one. This made peace between Council and Parliament but only just in time for both to face the Second World War, which of course prolonged the whole operation.

As the rebuilding of Waterloo Bridge became a reality the grandiose schemes for the rescue of Charing Cross from mediocrity and muddle faded. A Home Counties Traffic Advisory Committee in June 1936 reported in favour of safeguarding the future of such a scheme, entailing not only a great new combined road and rail bridge at Charing Cross but approaches stretching as far north as Euston Road and as far south as Elephant and Castle. The LCC, faced with an estimate of £32½ million for this, declared that it was '. . . more than the Council and the School Board together had spent on London Education since 1870!' and let the proposal die.

Sir Charles Bressey in his Highway Development Survey (1937), Greater London, effectively buried it: 'Owing to the quadrant curve of the Thames between London Bridge and Lambeth Bridge, all bridges radiate fan-fashion from what one may term "the handle of the fan" in the Elephant and Castle and St George's Circus neighbourhood—a notoriously congested area. To interpolate another spoke radiating from the same hub is a dubious means of relief.'

The new Waterloo Bridge was begun in 1937, over thirteen years after the old one had first given way—such was the price of controversy. Owing to the war and much interruption of the building operations by enemy bombing the new bridge did not come into partial use until 1942, and was finally opened in 1944. Sir Giles Gilbert Scott was the architect in association with the LCC Architect and Chief Engineer. Herbert Morrison wrote: 'The new and beautiful bridge was erected. Our argument that all good architects were not necessarily dead proved to be true. The critics came to admit our case. Waterloo Bridge is already one of the ornaments of the London scene—and a useful one, too.'

After its unprecedented service of eighteen years the timber of the temporary bridge had reached the end of its useful life but the girders and steelwork were carefully stored and packed. There were secret negotiations between the LCC, the War Office and the Ministry of Supply for its possible use in the invasion of Europe. After the capture of Antwerp it was duly shipped across the Channel and forwarded in special rail trucks to the front line. When the Germans, as had been foreseen, destroyed the Rhine bridges and the single bridge at Remagen had collapsed, the former temporary Waterloo Bridge was re-erected as a Rhine crossing—in the record time of just over seven days.

In the years of peace that followed, while there was a lull in the building and rebuilding of the tideway crossings, a single stirring event must be recalled. On a bright May afternoon in 1953 Major Christopher Draper, a sixty-year-old veteran of the First World War, took off in a hired monoplane and approached the Tower Bridge from the east as so many enemy raiders had done ten years earlier. The Major dived between the upper and lower spans of the bridge then went on to fly through Waterloo Bridge, Westminster Bridge and twelve other bridges to the west.

It was done to prove that he was still in possession of his faculties, and of course it led to his appearance at Bow Street Magistrates Court on eight summonses. Instead of a possible fine of £1,600 and six months' jail, the gallant Major was discharged conditionally on payment of ten guineas costs. 'I have been greatly impressed by the story of your gallant and splendid past and your difficult struggle against adversity,' the magistrate said. 'But this was a piece of folly which should never have been undertaken. . . .'

In the latter half of this century a significant new tideway crossing is the Dartford-Purfleet Tunnel between Kent and Essex. About seventeen miles east of London Bridge, this is a strategic crossing closely linked with the road systems already existing in the two counties. Its position and function have little to do with local residential needs. Though it is open for bicycles it does not cater for pedestrians. Its site between Dartford and Purfleet followed a survey by Sir Maurice Fitzmaurice in 1924 when the possibility of a Gravesend-Tilbury link was rejected. Essex and Kent County Councils jointly promoted the first Dartford Tunnel Bill in 1930 but construction was held off owing to the economic situation until 1936, when a pilot tunnel was started which was completed in 1938. The Second World War and subsequent economic difficulties prevented all further work on the tunnel until 1957, when the driving of the main tunnel began.

The tunnel was driven through water-bearing ground consisting of silt and gravel deposited by the river and the chalk lying beneath this alluvial material. To keep out ground water all work was carried out under conditions of compressed air. About 400 men were engaged, their working arrangements being governed by the latest knowledge of physiological problems involving divers and air crew. Regulations were well observed and there were no casualties. Finished in 1963 the tunnel carries a roadway of two traffic lanes and is just under 4,700 feet long. It is served by open cut approaches. It cost a grand total of just over £13,000,000, and the Dartford Tunnel Act contained authority for tolls to be charged; these, after deduction of operating costs, are devoted to payment of interest and reduction of capital debt. The schedule of tolls is

2½p	bicycles of all kinds other than powered variety
5p	motor cycles and motor cycle combinations
12½p	cars and goods vehicles under 20 cwt unladen weight
20p	goods vehicles above 30 cwt unladen weight with two axles
30p	goods vehicles above 30 cwt unladen weight with more than two axles

All collection of tolls is carried out on the Kent side of the river. A total of eight toll booths, four in each direction and situated about 800 yards from the entrance, deals with all traffic.

The gross income for 1970 amounted to £1,200,000. Though this makes good sense it is a reversion to former conceptions. Until the abolition of bridge tolls in the nineteenth century the river crossings were a charge upon the traveller's pocket. The re-imposition of a toll system to pay for public works is a trend in this country and in many other parts of the world where bridges and tunnels have recently been constructed.

Almost as soon as it was opened in the 1960s Dartford was working to capacity during the summer months. A duplicate tunnel is to be built in the 1970s.

Like the Tower Bridge the tunnel carries a permanent crew.

The administrative staff numbers 143, working in shifts with about twenty-eight men on each shift throughout every twenty-four hours. This means that any post requiring to be filled on a permanent basis needs four employees. There is an administrative building close to the toll booths on the Kent side containing staff messing and recreation facilities, since this station, so busy with cross-river traffic, is nevertheless curiously remote in itself.

In the control room the duty traffic controller presides, by closed circuit television covering the whole of the tunnel and its immediate approaches. The tunnel ventilating fans are also controlled by him, and to assist in deciding fan speeds the tunnel atmosphere near each entrance and in the central section is monitored for carbon monoxide content and smoke density. Vehicles entering the tunnel are counted by photoelectric cell equipment and the traffic controller can tell at any moment how many are in the tunnel. There is a system for adjusting the light level to prevent temporary blindness or dazzle. There are sophisticated fire-fighting and emergency breakdown arrangements, and Dartford was the first tunnel to draw up a comprehensive list of all dangerous substances carried on the roads of this country, with a copy of restrictions which apply to the tunnel. Vehicles with dangerous loads subject to these restrictions which have to be escorted through the tunnel are mustered into bays at the approaches. Thence several of them at a time are driven through in convoy with escorting patrol cars—Land Rovers carrying fire extinguishers of all types.

To keep traffic moving there is a minimum speed limit of 10 m.p.h. within the tunnel, and vehicles not capable of making this speed are banned except for slack traffic periods, when they may be escorted through the tunnel. Cyclists enjoy a unique service. Being themselves discouraged though not prohibited from pedalling through the tunnel, they are transported with their machines on Land Rover trailers capable of taking six cycles at a time. Though the cyclist only pays $2\frac{1}{2}$p in toll charge, the cost to the management of his journey averages out at over 20p. The tunnel authorities weigh this loss on the relatively few cyclists who use the tunnel against the risks and delays which could arise from cyclists going through under their own steam.

In 1970 a daily average of just over 23,000 vehicles used the tunnel.

A centenarian which needed attention during the sixties was the Grosvenor Railway Bridge serving trains into Victoria Station since 1860. The original bridge had been widened and improved three times during its life. In 1963 rebuilding began at a cost of over £2,000,000, the work taking about four years, during which the railway services were maintained in and out of the terminus.

15

'Build it up with Stone so Strong . . .'

Soon after it opened Rennie's London Bridge tilted noticeably downstream. A commission of engineers, including Thomas Telford, reported however that the bridge was entirely safe. Ever since, the bridge continued to sink slightly and unevenly and each year's inspection revealed a noticeable increase in the cracking of the masonry. While the basic superstructure was perfectly sound, it was estimated that the bridge was sinking into the river bed at the rate of one inch every eight years. This was no doubt due to the immense weight of the bridge—approximately 130,000 tons—combined with the increasingly heavy vibration of modern traffic. At each peak period 2,500 vehicles and 20,000 pedestrians were crossing the bridge. Announcing its demise and the fact that the Corporation of London would build and pay for a new bridge the Lord Mayor declared in 1967:

> This decision has been arrived at only after an exhaustive investigation into the possibility of incorporating the existing London Bridge in a scheme to provide the added width modern traffic now requires. This investigation has shown, without any reservation, that retention of the bridge, no matter how desirable, is structurally impracticable. This does not mean that the bridge has reached the end of its useful life—it is in fact perfectly sound. The reason is that due to its great weight, settlement of the timber foundations is now apparent and any major disturbance of these,

160

such as would occur in a widening scheme, would create a
structural hazard beyond the bounds of prudence.

The Corporation followed the unusual course of offering the
structure of Rennie's bridge for sale by tender and a form was
issued for the use of intending purchasers, beginning with the
words: 'We, The Undersigned, hereby offer to purchase and
remove materials resulting from the demolition of London Bridge
and stored at a quay-side site in Surrey Commercial Docks,
London, S.E., as described overleaf on this form of tender, and
subject to Conditions of Sale, for the sum of. . . .'

In this unique enterprise the Corporation made itself responsible for the cost of numbering and taking down all granite and
other materials. The granite was described as having 'weathered
well' and to be in good condition. 'However, stones broken during
demolition and any that are cracked or chipped can be replaced
by stones from other parts of the bridge structure subject to some
redressing.

'Each stone will be clearly marked with a number and a plan
prepared indicating the precise position of each numbered stone.
In addition, there will be photographs of particular parts of the
bridge, namely, a section of balustrading; a section of corbelling;
part of an arch face showing a number of voussoirs, and one of the
cutwaters.'

The Corporation's invitation for tenders received world-wide
publicity. A television news story carried it to Robert P. McCulloch, a Los Angeles industrialist who was conferring in a New
York Hotel with C. V. Wood, a designer who had been concerned
with Disneyland and Six Flags over Texas. McCulloch had been
scouting for test sites for his company's outboard motors in 1958
when he spotted a peninsula on Lake Havasu in Arizona and
planned for the site what he described as a 'carefully-grown city
with balanced economy, light industry and superb recreational
facilities'. To enhance the site he planned the cutting of a channel
which would turn the peninsula into an off-shore island. C. V.
Wood was his designer.

The news that London Bridge was for sale galvanized the two
men. The bridge would be the entry to their 'idyllic desert isle'.

So a successful bid was put in by the McCulloch Oil Corporation,
and a contract written in fine copperplate handwriting, unique
in its content and purpose, was drawn up between the Corporation and the 'Mayor and Commonalty and Citizens of the City of
London'. This memorable deal was set out in curiously decorative
style.

> *Whereas* there has been a bridge known as London Bridge across
> the River Thames for nearly two thousand years *And whereas* at
> the beginning of the 13th century the first stone bridge was built
> prior to which timber had been used to effect the crossing *And
> whereas* on the Fourth day of July One thousand, eight hundred
> and twenty three the Royal Assent was given to 'An Act for the
> Rebuilding of London Bridge and for the improving and making
> suitable approaches thereto' *And whereas* the foundation stone of
> the present London Bridge was laid by the Lord Mayor of London
> on the Fifteenth day of June One thousand eight hundred and
> twenty five and the bridge was formally opened on the First day of
> August One thousand eight hundred and thirty one by King
> William IV accompanied by his Consort, Queen Adelaide of
> Saxe-Meiningen *And whereas* the Corporation having decided that
> it is necessary to demolish the present London Bridge and to
> build a new London Bridge resolved to offer for sale the stone-
> work of the existing bridge elevations in a way which would allow
> its re-use as facings to a new bridge of similar shape and size so
> that the existing London Bridge which is an outstanding example
> of 19th Century skill in masonry design and construction is not lost
> to future generations *And whereas* in response to the Corporation's
> offer of sale the Purchaser has submitted a Tender dated the
> 3.26.68 to purchase and remove the materials resulting from the
> demolition of London Bridge for the sum of *Two Million Four
> hundred and sixty thousand dollars* of the currency of the United
> States of America. . . .

This agreement was duly signed on behalf of London by Sir
Desmond Heap, Comptroller of the Chamber and Bridge House
Estates and City Solicitor, the thirty-sixth in his line. Since the
deal was completed many American citizens have expressed
dismay on discovering that it was not the Tower Bridge which was
being shipped across the Atlantic.

The work of demolition went on smoothly into the 1970s, the
last shipment of Rennie's stonework crossing the Atlantic during
the spring of 1971.

Its successor, the new London Bridge, is a three-span pre-stressed concrete structure of 260 feet side span, with a 340-foot central span. The road layout provides dual three-lane carriage-ways. The design and construction were under the supervision of Harold K. King the City Engineer with Messrs William Holford and Partners as consultant architects and Messrs Mott Hay & Anderson, who had worked for the Corporation on Southwark, Blackfriars and the Tower Bridges, as consulting civil engineers.

There were special problems in the building of this first tideway bridge in the second half of the present century. The new bridge had to be built on the site of the Rennie bridge with the same access though it would be 40 feet wider. During the building the 20,000 morning and evening rush-hour pedestrians had to get across. It was a condition of the design that the bridge should be kept open to road traffic on all working days, and weekend and night closures kept to a minimum. There had to be minimum obstruction of river traffic—two 100-foot wide openings to be clear for navigation at all times—with maintenance of berthing facilities at adjacent wharves for both sea-going and river craft. The safety standards during deep pile-driving had to be observed, especially in respect of the Fishmongers' Hall, listed as an ancient monument and immediately adjoining the bridge, and the tunnels of the London Transport Board's Northern Line which run close to the north abutment works.

Construction and demolition were carried out in four stages:

1 Removal of the upstream footpath and construction of the upstream quarter of the bridge.
2 Removal of the downstream footpath and construction of the downstream quarter.
3 Demolition of the old bridge and construction of the centre two quarters of the new bridge.
4 Joining together the four quarters, designed as four box beams, and completion of the surfacing, kerbs and pedestrian barriers.

In the disused Surrey Commercial Docks a mile downstream a special casting yard was laid out where the segments of the new bridge were pre-cast. They made the short journey upriver by

barge and were hoisted into position by a special overhead gantry
built across the river.

The new bridge is supported on thirteen reinforced concrete
piles—four piles under each pier—constructed in shafts sunk more
than 85 feet into London clay. Parapets are finished in polished
granite with axed granite in the piers and abutments. The
spandrels of the arches are light grey in colour, using granite
aggregate concrete, and are illuminated by night. The cost of the
new bridge is £4½ million and it has taken just over 4½ years to
build.

While the rebuilding of London Bridge is a proud thing for the
citizens and for the nation, the Corporation did not rest upon that
accomplishment but set out to study once again the feasibility of a
new crossing—by a high-level bridge, bored tunnel or dredged
tunnel—to relieve the metropolitan pressures east of the Tower
Bridge. Sanction for the doubling of the size of the Dartford
Tunnel was a move to relieve the pressure of through traffic, but
no solution in itself to the traffic problems of the last quarter of this
century.

The present significance of the tideway as an obstacle rather
than a thoroughfare is shown in a GLC survey made in 1968. The
count covered road-crossings between Staines and Dartford—a
longer stretch than that covered in this book, with six more
bridges—and found that 780,000 passengers and nearly 450,000
vehicles crossed in each direction in a full twenty-four hours.
Between 1962 and 1968 cross-river traffic increased by 31 per
cent. Below Tower Bridge the increase during this period was 95
per cent, due largely to the opening of the Dartford Tunnel.

In spite of the works carried out upon the tideway the Thames
has not been wholly subdued. The 'strong brown god—sullen,
untamed and intractable' is still a force to be reckoned with.

Records kept of high water at London Bridge since 1791 show
that exceptional tides have been steadily increasing over the last
century and a half. In 1953 the flooding of the Thames estuary
and the East Coast caused the deaths of 300 people. If there were
a tide a foot higher than that of 1953, four times as much water
would come over and serious flooding would paralyse most of
London's main services and possibly 60 per cent of the under-

ground railway system. 'It may come as a surprise to many
Londoners,' wrote the GLC in a pamphlet in 1969, 'that their
benevolent River Thames can also be dangerous; to others this
has been perfectly clear for many years'.

The remedy of building a barrage or barrier to control this
menace has been a controversial issue for half a century. The
proposal which had won favour by the beginning of the 1970s
was for a barrier to be erected across the tideway in the Woolwich
area. This seems unlikely to offer crossing facilities, and this
perhaps is the best of all reasons for not enlarging upon it here and
adding to the already extravagant amount of literature on the
subject.

The Thames remains prodigiously important for its size, a
dimension of London, an axis from which the haphazard patterns
of the metropolis have arranged themselves. The crossings themselves are also somewhat haphazard, having followed local
expediency rather than strategic planning. They have not placed
the river in chains or in any way contained it. Their proliferation
and diversity belong to the character of Greater London. Their
adequacy may well fall short of London's traffic needs. But if the
river traffic ever returned and the tideway once again became a
noble, significant thoroughfare they present no obstacle to navigation.

SELECT
BIBLIOGRAPHY

Boucher, Cyril T. G.: JOHN RENNIE 1761–1821: THE LIFE AND WORK OF A GREAT ENGINEER, Manchester University Press, 1963.

Boulton, W. H.: THE PAGEANT OF TRANSPORT THROUGH THE AGES, Sampson Low, Marston & Co. Ltd.

Chancellor, E. Beresford: AN ACCOUNT OF THE BRIDGES ACROSS THE THAMES AT KEW, SURREY, Richmond, 1903.

Clements, Paul: MARC ISAMBARD BRUNEL, Longmans, 1970.
Clunn, Harold P.: THE FACE OF LONDON, Simpkin Marshall, Ltd, 1933.

Dickinson, H. W., and Titley, Arthur: RICHARD TREVITHICK, THE ENGINEER AND THE MAN, Cambridge University Press, 1934.

Ellis, Hamilton: BRITISH RAILWAY HISTORY, George Allen & Unwin, 1954.

Gibbon, Sir Gwilym, and Bell, Reginald W.: HISTORY OF THE LCC 1889–1939, Macmillan & Co. Ltd, 1939.

Herbert, A. P.: THE THAMES, Weidenfeld & Nicolson, 1966.

Home, Gordon: MEDIAEVAL LONDON, Ernest Benn Ltd, 1927; OLD LONDON BRIDGE, John Lane The Bodley Head, 1931.

Humpherus, Henry: HISTORY OF THE ORIGIN AND PROGRESS OF THE COMPANY OF WATERMEN AND LIGHTERMEN OF THE RIVER THAMES, WITH NUMEROUS HISTORICAL NOTES, 3 vols., (1874–6), London: S. Prentice, Printer, 47 Upper Thames Street.

Jefferson, E. F. E.: THE WOOLWICH STORY, published by the Woolwich & District Antiquarian Society, January 1970.

Lampe, David: THE TUNNEL, George G. Harrap & Co. Ltd, 1963.

Law, Henry: A MEMOIR ON THE SEVERAL OPERATIONS AND THE CONSTRUCTION OF THE THAMES TUNNEL BY SIR I. BRUNEL, 1857.

Lethaby, W. R.: LONDON BEFORE THE CONQUEST, Macmillan & Co., 1902.

Lewin, Thomas: THE INVASION OF BRITAIN BY JULIUS CAESAR, Longman, Green, Longman and Roberts, 1859.

Morrison, Lord, of Lambeth: HERBERT MORRISON, Odhams Press Ltd, 1960.

Rolt, L. T. C.: ISAMBARD KINGDOM BRUNEL, Penguin Books, 1970.

Sekon, G. A.: LOCOMOTION IN VICTORIAN LONDON, Oxford University Press, 1938.

Simmons, Jack: THE RAILWAYS OF BRITAIN, Routledge & Kegan Paul, 1961.

Walford, Edward: OLD AND NEW LONDON, 4 vols., Cassell & Company Ltd, 1890.

Walters, David: BRITISH RAILWAY BRIDGES, Ian Allan, 1963.

Welch, Charles: HISTORY OF THE TOWER BRIDGE, Smith, Elder & Co., 1894.

BRITISH BRIDGES, Public Works, Roads and Transport Congress, 1933.

Index

Index